/VIC BRADEN'S
MENTAL TENNIS

/VIC BRADEN'S
MENTAL TENNIS

How to Psych Yourself to a Winning Game

by Vic Braden and Robert Wool

LITTLE, BROWN AND COMPANY

BOSTON   NEW YORK   TORONTO   LONDON

First Edition

Library of Congress Cataloging-in-Publication Data

Braden, Vic.
   [Mental tennis]
   Vic Braden's mental tennis : how to psych yourself to a winning game / Vic Braden and Robert Wool. — 1st ed.
      p.   cm.
   ISBN 0-316-10516-3
   1. Tennis — Psychological aspects.   I. Wool, Robert, 1934–
II. Title.
GV1002.9.P75B72   1993
796.342′01′9 — dc20   93-7646

10 9 8 7 6 5 4 3 2 1

MV-NY

*Published simultaneously in Canada
by Little, Brown & Company (Canada) Limited*

Printed in the United States of America

To four nice people:
  Melody Braden
  Arthur Ashe
  LaVerne Moore
  Jack Kramer
            — VB

To my daughters, Vanessa and Zoë,
who are relatively new to tennis,
and to their remarkable mother, my wife Bridget Potter,
all of whom are extremely mental on the court and off.
            — RW

Acknowledgments

Our special thanks to Sharon Powers for her help in preparing this manuscript, and to Deborah Lohse for her effort in fact-checking the book.

— VB and RW

Contents

/ PART I

Understanding Your Mind,
Your Body, and Yourself
on the Court

CHAPTER 1

Four Concepts of Mental Tennis

Tennis is a psychological game.

People are always telling me that, and as a tennis coach and a licensed psychologist, I certainly agree.

But too often I find that what people really mean by that is "If only I could master the mental side of tennis, then it wouldn't matter if my strokes are lousy."

If you bought this book with that in mind, get your money back.

Life and tennis do not work that way.

You still need the strokes to play tennis well, but you will surely expand your capacity to develop those strokes and to play better if you can grasp the mental game. And you'll enjoy the game infinitely more as well.

For me, mental tennis embraces four concepts, all of which we'll consider in this book. If you can integrate them and apply them to your game, they will change the way you approach tennis. In fact, you will never play tennis quite the same way again.

Here's what I'm talking about:

1. *Mind-body connections.* Tennis is a mind-body sport, with one profoundly affecting the other. Your mind and body work together in surprising ways when you play. Under-

standing this relationship, how the brain/computer interacts with the neural transmitters, sensors, and muscles of the body, how software for each shot is created and encoded in the brain, how it can be altered — understanding all of that can enable you to change your technique, improve strokes, anticipate shots, even approach practice differently. That may be a lot to expect from one insight, but as we'll see in chapters 2 and 3, it is all possible.

2. *Psychological states, moods, affects, feelings, and problems all dramatically impinge on your game.* You don't need six years of psychoanalysis in order to hit a serve, but bringing to the surface, confronting, and understanding the anxiety and/or fear that overcomes you when you serve, or when you repeatedly double-fault, can allow you to become an effective server at last.

Mental tennis is also concerned with attitude. To improve your game, for example, you might well be thinking that there are seven separate adjustments you will have to make. That can be daunting, and can leave you feeling the whole effort is hopeless. However, from statistical measurements of several professional matches, tracking the number of shots each player hit on each point, I have discovered that lifting the level of your game might in fact be much simpler: for surprising results, hit one more ball back.

The more you understand yourself, the more you shed psychological baggage — whether it's anger on the court, collapsing under stress, the fear of failure (or of winning), as we'll explore in chapters 4 and 5 — before you get on the court, and the more you learn to cope with psychological crises that arise on the court, the better you will play.

3. *"Mental" implies "smart" and "intelligent" tennis.* That means understanding and incorporating good data into your game. Indeed, your game is only as good as your data. For a psychologist, this means acknowledging that what we see is often very different from what is actually happening.

To produce topspin on your forehand, for example, you do not flip your racket head over the top of the ball, as so many fans of Bjorn Borg started to do after watching the five-time Wimbledon champ hit his remarkably powerful topspin. They thought they saw him roll his racket over the ball. But that was not what he did at all. From high-speed film, I was able to reveal a quite different process, which we'll review in Chapter 11, and incorporating that data is what I mean by "smart" tennis.

This applies to your whole game. Measuring how you learn best, for example, and factoring that information into your choice of tennis instructors. Or confronting the great flat-shot myth. Jimmy Connors's shot might look as if it were clearing the net by only six inches, but actually the average with his deep shots is more like three or four feet over the net. Or, applying the law of gravity to your serve. A higher toss is by no means better.

As I think you'll see, data can be more than academically interesting. You might change the way you prepare to return serve, if you understand how your eye picks up the ball that's coming toward you and sends a message to your brain, and that it then takes the brain about 200 milliseconds — one-fifth of a second — to recruit the muscles to hit that ball. If tests also reveal that an 80 mph serve from your opponent reaches you in about a second, you can grasp how little time you have to prepare and swing. You have to begin to antici-pate that serve. And as we'll see, one of the ways you can do that is by picking up cues from your opponent, like where he makes his service toss, which signal where he is most likely to hit his serve.

Examining that kind of good data, as we will throughout this book, hopefully will lead you to abandon mistaken ideas you have held and cherished and to alter strokes that have been giving you trouble for years.

4. *"Mental" also implies strategies.* For many, to say that ten-

nis is a psychological or mental game means the obvious: a game of psyching out opponents and a game in which psychological forces are always playing upon us.

That's true, of course, but I'd expand the idea.

To me, "mental" also means working through the first three concepts above, and applying them to your game. That should allow you to discover new ways to approach opponents and matches, new kinds of game plans, new attitudes toward formerly difficult moments, new responses to common situations that now become programmed into your brain.

All of which should enable you to cut errors and play more efficiently.

Do that, and you'll enjoy tennis more than ever, and you'll feel better about yourself, too.

Nice combination.

/ CHAPTER 2

The Mind-Body Connection

ON THOSE DAYS when you found yourself hitting one backhand after another into the net, one forehand after another long, nothing but grief and frustration in the hot sun, the thought undoubtedly crossed your mind that tennis was not your game.

It simply wasn't meant to be, and since you are a fully grown adult, it probably never will be. And, furthermore, you told yourself with a sigh, you are a klutz, a dumb klutz at that. You've obviously learned nothing from all the lessons you've taken.

Allow me to offer extremely heartening news.

The reasons you are dubbing shots have little to do with your physical awkwardness, or your intelligence.

Chances are, you simply have the wrong software package in your brain.

Does that mean that if you change to the proper software, you'll be able to hit a respectable backhand?

Most likely yes.

And all you need to make the change are two pieces: an understanding of the model and the process — of your body and what it does when you play — and the willingness to practice the right way.

Let's start with the model and the process.

Your Brain, the Computer

Helen hits her dinky slice forehand crosscourt to your fore-hand, just as she has every Wednesday on this same Court 5 for years. Before the ball has barely left her racket, long before it reaches the net, your body anticipates it, knows what the shot is, and starts to move forward.

Your brain somehow knows that the shot will be short and will land somewhere around the service line. You reach a spot that will allow you to hit the ball on the rise, your body turns sideways to the net, and your right arm with the racket describes an arc, comes up the back of the ball, and continues skyward. As the ball, now spinning with the topspin you have put on it, heads for the open court, your body moves forward to the net, even though you can see that Helen probably will not get anywhere near your shot. She does not even try.

You have won the point and feel good about it. "Yes," you hiss to yourself. "When she gives you that short ball, move up and put it away."

At that moment of fleeting triumph, you might ascribe great powers to yourself. If you can keep playing like that, not only will you start to beat Helen regularly, but you are on your way to . . . who knows? The club championship?

Not to deny you your pleasure, but let's strip that point of its emotional elements, and in a somewhat simplified way examine its less glamorous mechanics.

Think of your brain as a giant computer, but one that is more sophisticated than any on the market. While the human brain remains too complex for anyone to understand completely all of its workings, we are able to monitor certain of its functions, including the way it sends signals to muscles.

When Helen hit her dinky slice, your eye picked up an image and transferred it to your brain. Since you have played with Helen for years, your brain translated that image even before she actually hit the ball. The way Helen brought her racket down from high to low in a chopping motion announced that this shot was going to be her familiar fore-hand slice. The brain processed the slice data and, drawing on its memory of that shot, recruited the muscles necessary to get your body moving forward, anticipating a short shot.

With the ball in the air, your eye picked up its image and passed additional data along to the brain: the relative speed of the ball, the kind of spin on it, its height, its direction.

Within approximately 200 milliseconds, one-fifth of a second, your brain has correlated all of this data and recruited the muscles necessary to hit the forehand topspin that will respond effectively to Helen's shot.

A winner, for which you do not give your eyes, your brain, or your muscles the slightest bit of credit.

Fortunately, you had the shot that was needed to put that ball away. Fortunately, in other words, your brain had that particular software package it could call upon. Though you don't realize it, you created that software and logged it into your brain over a period of months. It was during that stretch last year when you worked with your pro, over and over, on your topspin approach shot. Before then, you usu-ally took Helen's short ball and blasted it off the back fence, time after time after time.

In utter frustration, you finally turned to the pro and told him what was happening. "Let's work on it," he told you, and that's what you did. You told your friends during that time that after only a hundred years of playing, you were finally developing an approach shot that stayed in the court.

What was happening was this.

Some years before, you had learned how to hit that orig-inal approach shot. It was a shot you taught yourself around the time you expanded your game — when you started to venture from the safety of the baseline where you felt you had more time to respond to the ball and more time to get to it — to the more aggressive style of play that nearly all the best pros possess, the net game.

Quickly, you realized that a match against an opponent

was quite different from practice. In practice, you could position yourself at the net and volley one sharp winner after another. But in a match, you had to get yourself up to the net. So, the approach shot.

Perhaps because you had seen various pros hit the shot flat and hard — or at least it looked that way on your TV screen — you started to hit it that way as well. And, you discovered, when you got the shot in, it was either a clean winner or a very tough shot for your opponent to return. Also, it felt great to hit. Powerful. To be sure, you hit a lot of them long, but with time, you figured, you'd work out that little glitch.

So far as your brain/computer was concerned, you had begun to develop a software package somewhere between ten and twenty hits with that hard, flat approach shot.

If you had been wired up, you would have been able to see what is called a signature developing on the oscilloscope. The contraction of your muscles would begin to reflect your signature on the machine, and after some fifty hits, you could see a definite pattern.

Your signature for that approach shot, or for any shot, is extremely precise. In a typical experiment, my colleague and biomechanics mentor Dr. Gideon Ariel and I wired up one hundred students who all had essentially the same forehand. We registered their signatures with electromyography. Then I tried to trick that machine. I had student number 46 hit out of order. But a signature is so precise that the machine immediately identified the student as number 46.

Once the pattern is established — once the software is in your brain, in other words — it will stay there for decades. Not long ago, I was performing an experiment for the United States Racquet Stringers Association, trying to measure differences between nylon strings and gut. One of the tests was to compare the ball speed imparted by each.

I took two rackets exactly the same weight and make onto

the court, one strung with nylon, the other with gut. I was wired to record a number of responses. With the ball machine shooting balls at me, all at the same speed, I first hit ten with the gut, then, without missing a beat or a ball, I switched to the nylon. After the first ball with nylon, Dr. Ariel came running out of the lab.

"What happened?" he shouted. "What in the world did you do? With the eleventh ball, your signature changed."

I hadn't realized it, but I had a gut signature and I had a nylon signature. And even though I had not hit a ball with nylon for some thirty years, my brain still retained that nylon software, and when I switched rackets, I alerted my brain, and out came that old signature.

Similarly, you develop a signature for each shot, and you will hit each shot the same way. To oversimplify somewhat, if the image and data your eye transmits to the brain result in the brain's calculation that a backhand is required, it will retrieve the available software package for that shot and summon the required muscles.

There is a software package for each shot. There is one, for example, to make the ball rotate 30 revolutions per second, traveling at a particular speed on a particular axis. There's another to cause the ball to rotate 80 revolutions per second.

This is not to imply that if you summon the software to hit, say, a backhand, your stroke will yield the same result and go to the same spot every time. Tennis would be hopelessly mechanical if that occurred, but there is an important variable with each shot: the ball bounces differently each time.

You might also provide your own variable. In practice, you hit the backhand correctly a hundred times. But in the match, you hit it slightly off. What goes wrong? Anxiety, perhaps, as we'll see shortly.

To get back to your approach shot, you had a familiar

computer problem: garbage in, garbage out. You had created a software package that caused the ball to go long, time after time. You even laughed at your amazing consistency with the shot. You wanted to do something about it, had to do something about it, and that's when your pro said, "Let's work on it."

What finally happened was that you changed that software. You went through a process of motor learning in order to change your signature. It was not easy. It never is. But just think what this means: If you are willing to make the effort, you can correct any faulty stroke you have, even if you have suffered it for years. It means that you are not a prisoner of your past mistakes. You can develop wonderful new software packages for yourself.

The Struggle

However, if you are going to make the effort, you should approach the process with the understanding that the brain does not change a software package quickly. Normally, it takes about two months of fairly concentrated struggle, and that is why many players never correct fundamental mistakes in their game. They don't have the patience and the determination. They desire quick fixes. But the brain doesn't work that way.

As you discovered. It took a while to grasp the mechanics of the new approach, the footwork, the idea of hitting the ball while you were running forward. But before long, you did understand what you should be doing.

Yet, you didn't seem to be doing it. You seemed to be hitting your old shot, with somewhat different footwork.

Now your brain was resisting. It hadn't yet logged in the new software and meanwhile was sticking with your old package. As you persisted, however, trying to hit the new shot, as you used muscles differently and trained them, the brain picked up the elements, bit by bit, of a new signature for the approach shot.

Motor learning is quite different from intellectual learning. You read a book and there on one page is the answer you're looking for. "Great," you say, "I've got it. Now I understand." But in motor learning you might know what you want to do, but the brain replies, "Well, that's fine, but I've still got a package up here and I'm hanging on to it."

To make a change like this successfully, you need good information as well as a good learning environment, which usually means a coach who nurtures learning. Fortunately for you, for example, your coach knew the importance of the right kind of practice during this time. And you did it. Otherwise, it might have taken forever to change.

I've seen countless people trying to make such a change, but the only effort they make is when they are working on it with the pro. They have a lesson, and by the end of it, they are beginning to make some change, a short-term gain. Any good pro, at that point, will finish such a lesson with a warning and a plea. "This new approach shot might feel awkward every time you try to hit it," he'll caution. "But don't let that deter you. Between now and our lesson next week, just keep hitting it the way we've been working on it and you'll start to see results."

Invariably, what happens between the lessons is that people don't practice the shot the way it is supposed to be hit. And in the one match they play that week, after a couple of attempts at the new shot, without even being aware of it, they slip back into the old approach shot, the old software.

As a result, at the lesson the next week, they start out practically back at square one. They don't realize that unless they practice the new shot, unless they stick with the new shot, as awkward as it might feel, they are not going to develop the new software.

The same problem is widespread among skiers, as I discovered at my Ski College in Aspen, Colorado. Typically, a skier skis only a week a year. He starts out on Monday doing everything wrong. By Friday, even if he hasn't made a meaningful effort, he is skiing somewhat better, if still badly. The next winter, however, he's right back where he had been on Monday the previous year.

If, instead, he takes lessons and works on changing a motor skill, and skis enough during the week to begin to become comfortable with that new, unfamiliar signature, then the next year, by the end of the day on Monday, he's going to be where he left off the year before. He can build from there.

Making such a change is especially tough in our society, which, after all, encourages short-term gains. As you discovered, it was a real struggle, a struggle with yourself, a struggle to endure the discomfort of this new shot and to resist slipping back to the familiar. These difficulties feed the problems of many players, who unconsciously subvert their own efforts to change and improve. As we'll see in Chapter 4, they have a greater psychological stake in losing than winning.

I have long told my students that if the pain you suffer in not playing as well as you'd like and in losing matches is greater than the pain you suffer to make a change in your game, then your prognosis is terrific. But if the pain you suffer in making a change in your game is greater, then your prognosis is bleak. You are pretty well doomed to the frustration of repeating the same mistake over and over and over.

It often helps in this struggle if you can tell yourself that the change will not only remove pain from your game, it will add pleasure.

And, furthermore, it is a change that can last a lifetime. Once you change the software package, your game will never be the same, nor will you.

Beware the Stress Factor

After two months or so of practicing the new stroke, you begin to see on the oscilloscope that the new signature appears about 70 percent of the time. That means that on the court, the brain is now going to use the new software. But the old stuff is not yet erased.

Frequently, at a particularly stressful moment in the match, a tiebreaker for the championship and the big bucks, we see top pros get defensive. It's almost as if they regress back to the security of their old style, and you see old signatures creeping back into their play. But if they can block out that stress, then they should be able to hit the ball the way they are supposed to hit it, the way their new, improved signature will respond to it. Whether they are up 40–love or down 40–love, their signature on the oscilloscope should be the same.

The best players, like Rod Laver or Connors, are famous for their comebacks. We had a thrilling example of this from Connors in the 1991 U.S. Open. He was down five games to two and three match points in the fifth set to Aaron Krickstein, but he came back and won.

Connors hit every shot as he would normally hit it. Regardless of the score, his shot, his signature, would be the same.

Krickstein, on the other hand, under great stress, played it safe from the baseline. That might work with a lesser opponent, but against Connors — who thrived on such pressure and on being in such holes, who was a master at using the crowd to bolster himself in such situations — Krickstein should have known that he had to call upon another software package and go to the net. He had to force the play. Connors would not let him win otherwise. But Krickstein did not have that package to summon; he stayed at the baseline instead of forcing those final points at the net. So he lost.

We live or die by our software.

You might bear that in mind, the next time you take one of Helen's short returns on a big set point and, in a total regression to the old days, blast it off the fence. Rather than berating yourself and quietly cursing, pause and take stock.

Chances are you were not concentrating on hitting that shot the right way, the way you would hit it regardless of the score, if it were the first point in the match when there was no pressure, when you weren't thinking instead of how sweet winning was about to be.

You have to get your mind off the score. And the way to do that is to focus only on those elements that are important in stroking the ball.

If you do so, you will be able to connect with your new software package and off your racket will come that lovely, hard-earned topspin approach shot, a clean winner.

/ CHAPTER 3

The Mind-Body Connection on the Court

THE MATERIAL in the preceding chapter — the critical interaction between the brain and the body's muscles, and the way software is developed by the brain and called upon by it — is fairly dramatic stuff.

It is also extremely positive stuff, for it indicates that if you are willing to make the effort, you can develop just about any shot you need.

Unfortunately, that does not mean that in middle age you will suddenly be able to leap like a panther at the net. That involves genetics as well as reflexes, muscular development, and agility that may be ancient history for you and your body. But even if you cannot achieve your fantasy of resembling a combination of Boris Becker, Yannick Noah, and Mikhail Baryshnikov, think how much brighter life could be if you were simply able to hit a sharp volley with consistency.

There are any number of ways in which the mind and the body, the brain and the muscles, affect each other when you play. I'm sure you can verify many from your own tennis experiences.

For example, in the last chapter I mentioned the effect of stress on even the best players, causing them to revert to old software. Stress has other mind-body effects as well.

Just think about the times when you were up 5–2 against

a better player, yet you ended up losing. Just think about the times when you double-faulted on a big point, or when you had an easy volley at the net, a point that would give you a critical game, and you put it in the alley.

There are reasons for errors of that sort, under those pressured conditions. Let's consider those and a number of other common mind-body problems that we all face on the court, analyze what happens, and explore ways that you can begin to anticipate and deal with them. The best players in the world and absolute beginners share these problems.

Fear and Anxiety, Stress and Choking

"God, please let this serve go in."

Once again, you are pleading with the Almighty for intervention on your second serve.

Once again, on set point, as you sigh and gaze across the net at your opponent, who is performing his little bounce step just to remind you how ready he is to pounce on that ball, once again as you loosen your shoulder and prepare for the toss, you know you are going to hit this mother of all balls into the net.

"May as well get it over with," you say to yourself, and desperately make the toss, swing blindly, and watch it plop pathetically into the bottom of the net.

What an awful feeling that leaves you with.

First, of course, is the sense of abject failure. No matter how much you practice that rotten serve, no matter how well it seems to go during practice, when you are confronted with a big point in a match, failure seems inevitable.

What frustration. Nothing seems ever to change here. Nothing seems to make any difference.

What helplessness.

What impotence.

*　　　*　　　*

Choking is a universal problem, at one time or another afflicting the best pros as well as beginners.

Sports announcers continually remind us of the pressure on a player. Will he choke? Will she choke? The media reported that Ivan Lendl choked in the French Open of 1989 against Michael Chang. I think what happened to Lendl was more complicated than a simple choke, and I'll tell you why below. Certainly, there can be no denying that the stakes in that match were enormous, and the pressure on Lendl was great.

You might feel that this is a problem you need not be much concerned with. After all, when you play a match at the club, even a big match, there are not hundreds of thousands in prize money or millions in product endorsements at stake.

But, in fact, the finalist at the U.S. Open has a lot more in common with you than you might imagine. I've found that absolute beginners playing in their first tournament can be almost as debilitated from stress as Lendl, Navratilova, or Courier. Stress is stress. Blood pressure goes up. Your heartbeat accelerates. You might break into a warm sweat, then a cold one. Respiratory problems begin to surface. You might have trouble breathing or taking deeper breaths. Your pupils dilate.

In all these ways, your body and Lendl's are the same. The psychological stakes are the same for both of you. And stress can translate itself into powerful psychological forces.

I remember reading about a match some years ago between Miloslav Mecir, the masterful strategist from Czechoslovakia, and Jimmy Connors. This was one of Mecir's first big tournaments, and Connors, it turned out, was one of his idols.

Mecir beat Jimmy in the first set and most likely he couldn't believe it. But he was playing well, and in the second set, he had a big lead and was serving to close out the match.

All of a sudden he couldn't throw the ball up to serve. He could not serve the ball. He ended up serving underhand. Jimmy beat him in that set 7–5, took the next, 6–0. Here was one of the top players in the world serving underhand because, I'm sure, he suffered from mental/motor paralysis. Perhaps the idea of beating his idol was too frightening to him. What happens, after all, if you beat your father? Whatever the root of Mecir's problem, the result was that he froze, he was paralyzed.

I saw Vitas Gerulaitis play once against Rod Laver at Caesars Palace in Las Vegas. Vitas was a good player, but Rod was better, one of the best ever to play the game. And one of the most solid, psychologically. He was never rattled by being down in a match. Like Connors, he always remembered that he had to play a match shot by shot, and that the shot he was hitting at the moment was the only thing that mattered. Focus on that, he knew, and the score would take care of itself. He also knew how indifferent the ball was to the score.

So even though Vitas had Rod down, Rod kept hitting each shot, point by point, regardless of the score. The pressure mounted on Vitas to put him away, but he couldn't do it. And, with each point that Rod won, the stress on Vitas increased. In such a situation, you can get overwhelmed by a fear of loss of control and perhaps a loss of self-esteem. That fear of loss produces anxiety, and anxiety, as noted, can inhibit certain muscles from functioning.

Rod tied the match up and they went into a tiebreaker, which in those days was nine points. On the ninth point, Vitas served the first ball out of the court — *way* out of the court. On the second serve, he could get the ball only six inches out of his hand. He caught it and tried again. He double-faulted. He rushed straight to the locker room, disappointed with himself for losing that way, embarrassed at having choked.

Today, as a television commentator, Vitas not surprisingly is quite insightful on those moments when a player appears to be choking.

Stress, of course, does not have to come as a result of developments on the court. Often players bring stressful problems from the outside world onto the court.

I remember once in 1968, Butch Buchholz, one of America's best players at that time, came out to California to play in a tournament that I was helping Jack Kramer manage. Pancho Gonzales, the champion, had announced his retirement, and there was strong competition among Buchholz, Barry MacKay, Ken Rosewall, and others to become the new champ.

I arranged for Butch to use the home of friends in Malibu, and he came out with his puppy — he wanted to bring his new puppy, he had told me — a couple of days before the tournament. I went to the airport to pick him up in my Volkswagen, and I couldn't get this dog inside my car. This supposed puppy was bigger than my car. We had to put its legs together and slide it in sideways.

Butch had more than a day of practice for the tournament and he was working hard. As part of his preparation, he told me, he had even stopped smoking.

On the opening night of the tournament, as Buchholz's match approached, he was nowhere to be seen. He was so late that it began to look as if we'd have to disqualify him, when finally he came running in.

His puppy, he explained, had swallowed the car keys. So he had grabbed a cab in Malibu, but it was a union cab and it wouldn't go past Santa Monica. To cope with all this, he began smoking again.

Finally, he got out on the court against Lew Hoad. Hoad beat him in about forty-five minutes. It was the worst match I'd ever seen Butch play. Talk about stress — he had no idea where the ball even was. He was practically hitting the popcorn machine up in the second deck.

Recently, we had a vivid example of how pressure can affect a champion player, when Lendl played Chang in the round of sixteen of the 1989 French Open in Paris.

The pressure to win was all on Lendl. He was ranked number one in the world while Chang was then just coming up into the very top ranks.

Also, Lendl had to step onto that court not knowing very much about Chang's game and quite aware that he didn't know. Once a player has been around for a while, all the other players have a good book on him and they can generally anticipate what's coming. But with Chang, Lendl had little to go on.

Furthermore, match-ups in tournaments can be decisive. This was a tournament played on clay, and on clay, footwork is critical. You have to play on ball bearings, and Chang's major strength is his feet. He is one of the fastest players I have ever seen and can get to all kinds of balls. Drop shots, for example, are ineffective against a player like Chang. He not only can reach them, but also have time to do things with the ball. As a result, a lot of shots that Lendl was accustomed to hitting for winners were being handled deftly by Chang. And remember, Lendl had to learn and process a lot of fresh data as the match unfolded.

Factors like that will change the perspective and attitude of even a great player like Lendl. So, by the time Chang hit the famous underhand serve, they were no longer playing Lendl's game and he looked confused.

To make matters worse for Lendl, Chang got stomach cramps. That meant all the more pressure on Lendl to win.

It can be hard to beat injured people. I did a small study of matches at Forest Hills where the U.S. Championships used to be played, looking at the results of matches where players had minor injuries — sprained ankles and the like. In eight matches, the injured players all won. An injured player might be suffering a physical handicap, but he also enjoys a psychological advantage. It can be very tough to put that injured opponent away.

Also, various injured players including Stefan Edberg have reported after their lame but victorious matches that they found themselves concentrating ever more on their strokes, precisely to compensate for their injuries.

Jack Kramer had a clear view of how to cope with the injured-player kind of pressure. "Never get in a situation where you start giving games to somebody who's hurt or playing lousy," he said to me once. "If you like the guy and he's injured, beat his brains out as fast as you can and then go buy him a beer and a sandwich. Don't ever fall into the trap of giving people games, or letting up."

Let's get back to you and your anxiety or fear about serving.

That cold feeling blankets you every time you go to the line, especially on a big point.

What is it that disturbs you? An anxiety is different from a fear. Psychiatrist Rollo May put it nicely in *The Meaning of Anxiety:* "Fear is a specific reaction to a specific danger to which an individual can make a specific adjustment. Most fear is rational. Anxiety doesn't involve specific dangers to which you can adjust. It's difficult to put one's finger on the cause of anxiety, but it's easy to recognize the symptoms: a sudden appearance of dread, apprehension, terror, feeling faint. . . ."

If you get hit by a car while crossing the street, there is every reason for you to be fearful when crossing streets for some time afterward. But the source of an anxiety is not so apparent and specific. We all wake at times in the middle of the night, cold, sweating, anxious, yet there is no one standing there in the bedroom with a gun, nor for that matter has there ever been. You cannot at first be clear about the cause of an anxiety, but you can trace it. You may not be able to describe it precisely, but usually you suffer a feeling of uncertainty and the premonition that something bad is about to happen.

After interviewing hundreds of professional and amateur players, I believe that choking is usually a manifestation of anxiety, rather than fear. The cause is unknown, or at least not apparent. Certainly there is nothing in the immediate reality to cause it. Your opponent is not pointing a gun at you, is he?

Choking so often occurs in predictable situations: the second serve on big points; ground strokes when you're up a couple of games; volleys on key points.

When you choke and feel caught in a cycle of repeated failures, to break the cycle, you've got to be your own analyst. You've got to pause and reflect on what's happening. What are you feeling? Why does this particular point seem so forbidding to you?

You'd be amazed at what you can do about serve anxiety if you confront it when it surfaces, if you pause and take note of what you're feeling.

Losing a match, or self-esteem?

Ask yourself what it is that you dread. Is it losing a point in a tennis match? Of losing a whole game? Sure, you're out there sweating and moaning and doing all you can, and in return you'd like the reward of winning. But, in the grand scheme of life, if you lose, how much can that matter? It surely doesn't make you a lesser person, does it? Or does it?

Some people have found it useful to fill in the blanks. "If I lose this serve, I lose the match. If I lose the match, then I lose _____ . If I lose _____ , then _____ will happen."

Suppose you apply this to your own serve anxiety and upon honest consideration fill in the first blank with the word "self-esteem." Okay, you are discovering and admitting to yourself that you have quite a bit invested in a tennis match, that you are actually going to think less of yourself as a human being if you lose a tennis match.

That's quite a discovery. It means that, in fact, you are not out there to use your body well, to enjoy the sun and a friendly match, to improve your net game. You are out there to demonstrate how much better and more powerful you are than your opponent.

From that perspective, with that motivation, if you lose, I can understand how you might feel that loss personally.

I am not speaking theoretically here. Frequently, I do find when I talk to people about their choking that their anxiety stems from a fear of losing self-esteem. In close, match-deciding moments they begin to worry that if they lose the match, they will lose the admiration, friendship, love of people who matter greatly to them.

But if we step back and put the anxiety elements into perspective, we see that all we are talking about is a tennis match, a crummy tennis match. Okay, you might lose it, but in terms of what really matters in life, what can one lousy tennis match really mean? Everybody loses matches, even the best players in the world. And you are going to lose a lot more in life than tennis matches.

If we reflect on that concern for the loss of self-esteem and self-respect, the loss of admiration and love from friends, it should soon become clear that if someone only wants to be around you or likes you because you win tennis matches, then that person isn't a real friend anyway. Why do you need that kind of phony friendship and false admiration anyway?

Maybe, then, you have to sort out these motivations and objectives. A writer told me once of an enormous insight he had gained through psychoanalysis: If someone criticized his writing, that person was not criticizing him as a human being. To have one of his books battered by critics still hurt, but the blows were not to him, personally. Those reviews did not make him a lesser, rotten person. They were, after all, reviews of the book, not of him. The critic was responding to the book itself, most likely had never even met him. The critic's remarks could not then be personal. Once he grasped and absorbed this, he was able to accept criticism rather dispassionately. If a critic made a reasonable point, he could weigh it, perhaps even make use of it in his next book. If the critic was clearly off the mark, or perhaps his views were distorted because of his own problems, he could simply toss the review aside with a shrug.

Do you really intend to invest so much of yourself in a tennis match? Or did that happen without your realizing it? Did it happen unconsciously? Is it an extension of the way, perhaps, you approach everything?

More to the point, now that you have a fuller picture of what's happening, of where the anxiety flows from when you go to serve on a big point, do you want to try to change the dynamics? Could you, for example, as the writer did, separate your self-worth from a tennis match? Could you, with your new insight, approach the game of tennis with newly directed motivations? Could you, for example, try to remember that, in fact, tennis for you is only a game?

Or, to consider another unconscious problem I have often seen: Do you have a fear of *winning* the set, the match?

Be honest with yourself. Sit down after the match and think about it. Make notes to yourself. Are you really suffering from a fear of winning? Do you fear that if you start winning, you will be expected by peers or authority figures to continue winning, and that is too great a strain on you? What do you think will happen to you if you do beat this opponent? Do you have some reason for denying yourself the pleasure of winning the match? Do you have some reason for punishing yourself, for repeating this pattern of torture on one big point after another?

Perhaps the source of the serve anxiety lies elsewhere. For example, people often tell me they feel a sense of disapproval when they double-fault. And I have to ask: Disapproval by whom?

Frequently, what I find with people who choke is a childhood connection, perhaps some distant parental conflict that surfaces. There is, for example, some haunting fear that a loss of a tennis match will mean a loss of parental love, a fear so great that it cripples. Perhaps the fear was actually experienced years ago, yet the trauma lives. We all have a need for parental approval that lingers even long after we are parents ourselves. Is that what is haunting you when you serve for a big point?

I can't tell you the number of parents of young competitors I've seen who tie their approval to their child's success on the court. Often, they do it unconsciously, so neither the parent nor the child is aware of it. But that doesn't make it any less real, any less felt by the child when he or she loses in the quarter-finals.

Or you may be affected by some other anxiety, some other residue from childhood. As I said at the beginning of the book, you don't need six years of psychoanalysis to be able to hit a serve. But it is amazing what you can do for yourself if you use some of the tools of analysis to figure out what is haunting you.

Try not to deny the feelings that surface. To the contrary, welcome them. They can be the clues that enable you to discover what is really happening. Make a mental note when it happens. Think about it later after the match. Start a private notebook. You can trace the patterns more easily that way.

But merely surfacing the anxiety and confronting it will go a long way to releasing you from that problem and allowing you to hit a serve without obstructions, freely.

To be sure, many people do not want to surface such fears and feelings. "I don't need a lot of psychological junk to hit a good second serve," they say. "I just need a new grip."

I understand that attitude, and when I encounter it, I respect it. But unfortunately, most often they need more than a new grip, and by denial those people are pretty well doomed to repeat, to be hostage to their choking anxieties.

Also, they are losing an opportunity. Choking can be a signal that there's something stirring in you that you were previously unaware of. It's an invitation to explore yourself, to learn more about yourself. What is greater than self-knowledge?

You don't have to share your examination and your discovery with anyone if you don't want to. You'll be exploring the most personal and private matters, and you might not feel comfortable sharing them even with your spouse.

That doesn't matter. By surfacing the material, by facing the problems and the patterns they seem to project, you can provide yourself with new insights. Simply going through the whole analytic process can be sufficient to dispel the trouble — and the choking along with it. In other words, by recognizing that the problem has nothing to do with the mechanics of your serve or the strength of an opponent's ground strokes, but rather is connected to the fear that goes back to childhood of not being successful enough, of not being good enough to deserve the love of your parents — as tenuous as it might seem — that recognition can allow you to dissolve the problem. After all, you can then see that you are no longer a child playing to win affection. You are an adult, perhaps an adult with children of your own now, and in fact you are playing for your own pleasure on a lovely, sunny Sunday morning.

I am oversimplifying somewhat, of course. You might not be able to uncover the stuff that's causing you such choking grief. The roots might be too deeply buried to be surfaced without the help of a therapist.

But try. I have seen people do it, just as I describe. The

more they do it, the better they get at it. And the rewards are great.

They stop choking.

They also rid themselves of related anxieties, the sense of failure and frustration that pursues them off the court, and that can be debilitating long after the match.

Another approach to the serve problem

Try the process of self-analysis when you find yourself choking repeatedly under the same or similar conditions.

In addition, if your problem actually is double-faulting under pressure, there's another, psychologically less complex, effort you can make: work on a second serve. The results could be more than you imagine, including an unexpected, subtle psychological one.

Quite simply, if you go into a match with a modest but dependable spin serve working, having practiced that serve to the point where you feel some confidence in it, you will probably find your first serve improves as well.

In a sense, this is what happened with Stefan Edberg a few years ago. He decided that his second serve was weak, so he called upon CompuTennis, a company that analyzes tennis matches with computer compilations. It provided him with data on that second serve, which it had gathered from matches over the previous year.

To Edberg's great surprise, the study by statistician Bill Jacobson showed that Edberg had won about 80 percent of his second-serve points, a phenomenally high percentage. Once he reviewed that data, he knew that for whatever reasons, his mind was playing some trick on him. What he thought of as a soft spot in his game was nothing of the sort. Relieved, knowing just how good that second serve really was, he was then able to hit his first serve with more confidence than ever before, since he knew he had such a strong second one to fall back on.

You might not possess the high-bouncing super twist of Edberg, but the same principle of psychological confidence can work for you.

Blasting through the choke

There are times in tense matches when your opponent comes to life and lifts his game. Perhaps his shots are causing the match to shift his way. On the other hand, you might be helping his effort by choking. If you suspect yourself of collapsing yet again, there is a mechanical adjustment you can try that often helps: Blast away.

When you are choking with ground strokes, you are being tentative, fearful of hitting solidly. You are being passive, probably doing too much thinking. You are sending mixed messages to your brain, calling for a new signature.

To break that pattern, even as it is forming on the court, swing hard.

Not wildly, but as hard as you normally swing. How often you've heard Connors or McEnroe yell at themselves, "Hit the ball!" They know that they're choking and they have to break out.

You might hit a few shots long, but you give yourself a chance to be active and aggressive again, to get back to the signature you used when you were winning. You give yourself a chance to break the choking pattern.

You can also help yourself by focusing on the mechanics of what you have to do. Perhaps with the serve it is your toss, or the grip you want for the spin on the second serve.

Your problem might be return of serve. Coldly analyze it. The server is hitting a hard serve. You have to take another step back. You have to anticipate better, to concentrate on the cues his body gives off so you can predict where he is going to hit the ball.

Once again, by focusing on mechanics you will deflect emotional content from the moment. You will not fall victim to motor paralysis. Instead, you will be able to send messages to your brain that will allow you to hit the ball correctly and not reinforce your mounting doubts.

Distractions and External Stimuli

"Concentration" is a word that is thrown around a great deal in tennis and by tennis commentators.

Actually, researchers have a lot of trouble agreeing on what it means. On one level, certainly, it means being able to focus totally on the task at hand, on proper execution.

One form of this total engagement is known as "playing in the zone." You might think from the way it's used that the reference is to some particular section of the tennis court, probably one you have never seen yourself. And frequently when tennis players are asked to describe what they mean by playing in the zone, they are not very illuminating. "I was floating on a cloud. . . . The ball seemed so big, like I couldn't miss. . . . It didn't matter what I did, the ball went in."

What happens at these times is that the player is so immersed in his game that all external stimuli are blocked out. Mind and body are fused and functioning automatically to perform in a most efficient, productive, and effective way.

External distractions can at times be pretty silly. I remember, for example, playing doubles in a charity match in Florida. My partner was Anita Bryant. We were playing against Bobby Riggs. His partner was an elephant.

Originally, Bobby's partner was a dog. But they didn't get along and the dog bit Bobby, so he changed partners. Then he was tied to this elephant.

People say that elephants are dumb, but having played against one, I don't think they're so stupid. For example, if I threw up a lob, that elephant would just back up one step. Bobby would rush back five. It was really quite a smart animal.

To be sure, it was the only elephant Anita or I had ever played against. I guess my point here is that you might think playing against Bobby Riggs and an elephant would be pretty easy. That we'd wipe the court with them, as it were. But we were so distracted, we couldn't play worth a nickel. You would think we could jerk Bobby all over the place, have him continually running into the elephant or trying to pull the elephant around the court. But it was amazing how many balls we missed.

To be sure, in most matches you won't find yourself playing against an elephant, at least not a four-legged elephant. But I think you get the idea that it is easy to be distracted by external stimuli.

Perhaps a better example is found in how you respond to a bad line call, especially in a close match. How it affects your concentration.

So many people have a tendency to lose a match, let it slip away, when they get what they consider a bad call in a tight situation. To some degree, I think a lot of these people are really looking for an excuse to lose (as we'll see in the next chapter).

There's another kind of external stimulus worth noting that doesn't come from the events directly unfolding on the court. A good example of this was the way Billie Jean King's enthusiasm could inadvertently plant external stimuli in the thoughts of other players.

At one point during the tour in the late 1960s, Billie Jean told us all that she had been working with Australian pro Mervyn Rose and he had taught her a new forehand. The results, she maintained, were miraculous.

I watched her and I was puzzled by this supposed transformation, so I shot footage of her hitting it. What I saw, shooting 64 frames a second and comparing her new forehand with her old, was that Billie Jean looked apprehensive as she hit that new one. As before, she produced the same grimace just before connecting with the ball. From the film, I could not see much change on the stroke. She had a new approach, but at the point of impact on the shot, it looked to be the same old forehand.

What mattered, however, was her tremendously positive attitude. She believed that it was a new forehand and she excitedly told everybody on the tour that it was new and better than ever. And they believed her.

So, rather than looking at the ball, they listened to what Billie Jean had to say. The result was that her regular opponents got it in their heads that Billie Jean, who had been tough enough before and was already ranked number one in the world, now had yet another weapon, an even better forehand.

Intruding Forces

Over and over, I tell my students that they must concentrate, they must focus on each shot. If they can do that and execute properly, I tell them, they will be successful and winning tennis players.

What I mean by "concentration" is focusing on only what you must to recruit the right muscles to hit the needed shot. Or, to put it differently, focusing on whatever it takes for you to execute properly.

Sounds simple. But what happens when you are on the court trying to concentrate, and your mind becomes cluttered with noncourt matters?

I have identified thirteen different forces that impinge on professionals when they play a tournament, including the media, tournament sponsors, endorsements, business managers. These and other forces intrude on their moods and thoughts while they are playing a match.

Pros also have to relate to several authority figures — the

linespeople, the umpire, the tournament referee — and for some people authority figures get transposed into parents, everyone's original authority figures.

What, after all, explains the disproportionate rage that a player hurls at an umpire? What explains the childish tantrums that we often see with players?

A player has every right to appeal a call. But in my view, the temper tantrums and the cursing and threatening of the umpire are often related to something else, to the player's attitude toward a parent or authority figure.

A player who has problems coping with authority figures can be overwhelmed. After all, how can you concentrate on your strokes when you feel that you have been betrayed once again by your father or your mother?

Peers Impinge on Us

If you are worried about the score of the match, worried about having to face friends at the club and tell them that you lost, then you will not be able to focus.

As soon as you start thinking more about the score than your shots, you are on the way to losing.

If you find yourself being affected this way, try to track it. Try to note when this happens in match, when such worries intrude, become palpable. That awareness will help to alert you to the process as it recurs.

Peer pressure of this sort won't disturb you, if you are comfortable within yourself, if you know why you're playing, what you're trying to achieve that day. If you know that you've made a nice effort in that match, the prospect of facing a friend who asks, "Did you win?" won't disturb you or your concentration. You are playing for yourself. Within yourself, you can answer: "Nope, lost the match, but won my battle."

Tips toward Concentration

If you're going to be good in tennis, or at anything, you must learn to focus only on those elements that are important to you and your success.

Concentration for our purposes means ruling out external stimuli. However, you do not concentrate, or should not try to do so, by reminding yourself to concentrate.

In terms of the way your brain functions, if you have to surface the command and tell yourself, "Concentrate," then you are focusing on the command to concentrate, not on the game.

There are, however, a number of techniques you can use to improve your concentration on the court.

- First of all, as I noted above, stop thinking about the score or potential score. Think about the next ball that has to be hit and what you want to do with it.
- Concentrate on the job at hand and don't overload your brain with too many tasks. It is enough to focus on where you want to put the ball without simultaneously worrying about the perfect grip, the perfect swing, the perfect body position.
- Concentration is directly related to preparation. How you practice during the week will greatly affect how you feel about your game. If you are anxious about, say, your backhand, chances are you will be thinking about the weakness of that stroke when you go to hit it in a match, and not be able to concentrate on the way you want to hit the shot itself.
- Do your homework. If you do, you are going to be infinitely more relaxed when you get out on the court. Before a match, think about your opponent. If it's a club match, chances are you've played this person before. You know something about his or her game. You know that she never comes off the base-

line, which means that you may want to force her to come in toward the net. You want to run her.

The more you prepare and watch someone play, the more cues you can log into your brain. The more you think about how she's going to hit a shot, the more certain you will be that she is going to hit a particular shot against you in a particular situation. You will be able to think like a world-class player: you will be able to anticipate shots.

If you know that you really have prepared for the match, you can rule out that terrible feeling of uncertainty that would otherwise be there, that rushes up when you come out on the court, hit a few balls with an opponent, and suddenly start wondering, "Does she have a strong backhand? . . . How does she move?"

• Some people make a list of strokes, of points about their game they want to remember. And they review the list before they go out on the court.

Arthur Ashe used to put a note under the umpire's stand. It said, "Move your feet," a constant reminder to him to keep moving and not go flat. It's a good tip for all of us.

• Before a match, I like my students to put together a game plan and an alternative and discuss them with me. How do they intend to play this person? What are they going to do with what shots at what point in the match? I talk to them about exactly what circumstances will cause them to turn from Plan One to Plan Two. I want them to think about that ahead of time. The brain does not seem to like a lot of surprises during competition.

I also ask them to write down the most important three, four, or five points they want to accomplish out on the court. Not what they want to achieve off the court. This has nothing to do with rankings. It has to do with playing shots. So, for example:

1. Start early. Get as early a start as I can for the shot.
2. Know where I'm going to hit the ball.
3. Anticipate my opponent's shots.

Write that sort of instruction down and repeat those points to yourself between points and games, or during the exchange of sides — it's too tough to do any of this conscious thinking in the middle of points. But, do that and you will stay focused on the ball, the point, the match.

Self-doubt

"I just knew I was going to double-fault."

The interesting question to me about this pervasive problem is: Does the brain have a software package for double-faulting? I think it does.

Look at the process. Once you are ready to serve and the idea of double-faulting is in your mind and the image of double-faulting is on your brain, you are going to double-fault. If you send that wrong message to the brain, it will cooperate by contracting the muscles that cause you to double-fault.

I found the same problem with any number of beginning skiers at my Ski College. When somebody got the idea into his head that he was going to fall, he began to say to himself, "I'm going to fall." And that would almost guarantee that he would contract the muscles necessary to make himself fall, a pretty vivid example of mind-body interaction.

To cope, we suggested to skiers a very simple technique: If you find yourself saying, "I'm going to fall," counter that by saying, "I can make it . . . I can make it." Interestingly, this worked over and over. It was a matter of sending a positive picture to the brain and recruiting the right muscles.

We've done a number of tests with people wired up with EMGs, electromyography sensors, to measure responses. In one of these tests, we asked a high hurdler to imagine himself actually running a high hurdle race. Sure enough, we began to see faint muscle contraction patterns that matched those used for leaping over high hurdles.

So try to remember that the image you have of what is happening or who you are is very important in terms of what muscles you contract. If your image is one of failure, you are going to increase your chances of failing considerably. It is very hard for the brain to get the message "I cannot do it," and then be able to contract the muscles that will permit you to do it. The brain can send only one program at a time, so it's difficult for it to generate a success and a failure package simultaneously. If you say you cannot hit that ball, then you are pretty well guaranteeing that you are going to contract the muscles that assure that, in fact, you do not hit that ball.

Unfortunately, simply telling yourself that you can hit the ball does not guarantee you a winner. Merely projecting a positive image to the brain is not sufficient. You may not have the right stroke in your repertoire, the right software package at the brain's disposal.

I have seen countless people come off the court quite frustrated because of this. They are trying, really trying, they tell me, keeping a truly positive attitude, but somehow they still make so many errors. Alas, these stout souls do not yet have the strokes and the engineering to go with their psychological message. They might, however, enjoy extremely rich fantasy lives.

Self-doubt and Self-fulfilling Prophecies

Self-doubt is going to cost you more than a serve. It has a way of spreading, of becoming a cyclical and destructive process.

It may start with an anxiety-ridden double-fault, then lead to a couple of easy shots you turn into unforced errors. Soon, you are saying to yourself, "I simply cannot do this. I'm just a klutz and I cannot move fast enough to get into position to hit a proper backhand."

If you succumb to this, you're going to start missing more and more shots.

We can learn something from great players that will definitely help you resist the degenerative self-doubting process, but first a caution: You are never going to perform error-free. You are always going to commit mistakes. Expect that. It is only human. Your entire tennis game, not to mention your life, will improve if you keep that in mind.

Great players respond to their momentary failures and mistakes on the court by pushing and willing themselves toward mental recovery. They never submit to the cycle of self-doubt, the cycle that starts with a silent cry, "I'm finished!"

Jimmy Connors is a fine example, and not only because of his comeback in the '91 U.S. Open. Throughout his long, remarkable career, he has played with the same attitude: If he makes a mistake, he makes a mistake. Then he moves right on to the next point. He plays each shot as it comes along. He is imbued with the transcendent wisdom that the ball doesn't know what the score is; the ball doesn't care who's hitting it. All he has to do is concentrate on hitting that ball correctly.

In that sense, to Jimmy, it does not matter what the score is. He might well be down, say, 5–3 in the set, and his opponent thinks, "Wow! I've got him 5–3. If I can just hang on, I win the set." As soon as that player thinks such thoughts, he unconsciously alters his style of play.

Meanwhile, Jimmy is not muttering to himself, "Gee, it's 5–3 — if I lose the next game I lose the set, so I'd better watch it." No, he plays the ball, each point, the same way, the way he thinks it has to be hit. It does not matter to him what the score is. And half the time that is why he wins. His opponent starts playing conservatively and Jimmy is hitting the way he always hits.

Connors also knows when he has to change his style of play, and perhaps even more important, when to manipulate the crowd in order to wrest control from his opponent. That was what the Connors fight against Aaron Krickstein at the 1991 U.S. Open was all about.

As I noted, Krickstein was beating Jimmy in the fifth set and was up 40–love, but Krickstein was incapable of playing more aggressively, of going to the net and forcing Jimmy to pass him.

When Jimmy won a point, making it 40–15, the crowd started cheering for him. As soon as Krickstein heard that, he must have had his doubts. After he lost a second point and heard an even greater roar, the game was over, and I think that both players knew it.

I have seen Connors down countless times like that and then defiantly use his position to put more pressure on his opponent, brazenly challenging his opponent to close out the match.

Anger

For most players, anger is costly.

Whatever causes the flush of anger, perhaps even a tantrum — a bad line call, an opponent who is cheating, disgust with the way you netted an easy overhead — the effect normally will distract you from the game, and drain your energy and concentration. When most people have an angry fit, their game disintegrates, and quickly.

Anger not only drains you, but it puts you in a frame of mind that can easily lead to errors, discouragement, and defeat. Indeed, some players who have a need to lose use anger as an excuse for doing so. It's a perfect excuse.

With anger, you get distracted from the game, as emotions flood into your mind. Now you are not so much playing tennis as searching for an emotional outlet. Rather than concentrating on what has to be done to win a point, you might, for example, decide that you are going to murder your opponent. Not just beat him, but murder the poor slob.

So you try hitting harder than before. You have decided that you are going to put away every shot.

Unfortunately, nobody can put away every shot. The result will be a lot of balls going into the net and off the back fence. And the more points you blow, the angrier you get, until finally you are totally disgusted with yourself and the game of tennis itself. "What am I doing out here anyway?" you ask yourself. "I think I'll take up volleyball."

If this is happening to you, approach it the way I suggested you approach serve anxiety. Confront it. Make a mental note when the anger surges. Reflect on it after the match.

Often, anger covers hurt. Does that fit with your emotions? Why are you berating yourself so severely? Why are you exhibiting yourself in public as a child? Temper tantrums, after all, are typical of children and adolescents, not adults.

As with severe anxiety, ask yourself what the loss of a point, a game, a match really means to you. What have you invested in this supposed game?

If you need motivation, you might do what a woman working with sports psychologist Jim Loehr did: watch yourself on tape. For her, it was a profound revelation. Until then, she had no idea what she looked like during one of her famous fits. But once she saw the tape, she was so appalled by the way her anger transformed her, the grotesque way it made her look, she monitored herself and would not allow herself to be possessed by anger on the court again.

If that doesn't work for you and you have a pattern of uncontrollable outbursts, then perhaps you should explore your anger with a therapist. After all, if the anger keeps exploding, quite clearly you have a problem that is not limited to the tennis court.

Conversely, if it is your opponent who throws a fit, you should recognize that you could have a great opportunity. Her fit means that she is on the edge, and basically all you have to do to win is reduce your errors and play steadily (which is not the same as "hanging in there").

With her anger, she will have a tendency to want to win points quickly. But, by playing steadily, you're going to force her to earn every point.

Meanwhile, her anger will act as a stimulus, making it more difficult for her brain to recruit the appropriate muscles. A stroke with a lot of racket head play that requires a 15-millisecond response time is not going to work right any longer. And when that happens, she will begin to develop self-destructive, self-fulfilling prophecies. She is angry. And she feels she's right.

Emotional Opponents

The disturbing emotions unleashed during a tennis match may not be coming from your inner reaches. They might very well be stimulated by your opponent.

Frequently, the better you play, the more problems you will cause to surface in your opponent. That's when he starts to holler and curse. "What's wrong with me? . . . I cannot believe what's happening out here. . . . I'm getting worse with every shot."

That kind of outburst can be upsetting, not only for him, but for you. Try to remember that you can only handle what's going on on your side of the net. You don't have a clue to what's really happening to your opponent, and it is not going to help you to become enmeshed in his problems. Above all, you should not be distracted from your game by his antics.

If you find that you are, check yourself and ask, Why? Are you looking for a way out of this match? Are you perhaps upset with the judges, the same ones he is screaming at? Be careful that you don't displace the anger you might have for the officials upon yourself.

Repeatedly, we see that people playing against McEnroe get ensnarled in his problems and they pay dearly for it. I am convinced that McEnroe uses his own anger at times to pump himself up, at other times to distract and manipulate his opponents.

Recently, in his new role as television match analyst, he gave us, unintentionally, an insight into his motivations for such behavior. Speaking of a player on the court who was acting up as if he were, of all things, John McEnroe, he said: "He'll really milk this one to get the crowd on his side."

Such tactics became ingrained in his play at least partly because the rules appeared to permit his actions. Only once was he thrown out of a major tournament. Otherwise, he was encouraged loudly by fans and subtly by a few tournament directors who believed that ticket sales increased when Mac behaved that way.

When you find yourself against a McEnroe-type player, recognize what is happening. Most likely, you are being presented with an opportunity. Your opponent is in trouble. When he's winning, he doesn't throw fits of this sort.

It is possible he might be trying, as Mac does, to throw you out of your rhythm and off your game because something is not going right for him. But McEnroe is nearly unique in the way he can use that play.

Whatever is motivating him, don't get involved. When I see a player stop and start to listen to Mac, even drift over to the umpire to get a better view of the show, I know that player is in trouble.

Instead, he might take advantage of this rest time. It's really a bit of a gift. He could do some breathing exercises to relax, talk to the ball boy, grab a couple of balls and practice his serve. Anything but become a spectator or a participant in his opponent's show.

If a player lets Mac take him on an emotional roller coaster, he has fallen into Mac's trap. Same for you. Let your opponent berate himself and everyone around him, scream and holler. Keep yourself disengaged. It's too deep an issue for you to figure out why he's gone berserk.

If you can distance yourself and play in the same manner you were playing, the way that so unhinged him, you might win this match, and rather quickly.

Handling Cheaters

"Just out" may be the two most abused words in tennis.

We have all suffered cheaters, people who consistently call any close shot out. And we have all played against perfectly well-meaning, honest people who make inaccurate calls over and over. So it's best to be prepared for your share of bad calls. Jack Kramer told me he expected at least six bad calls a match from the umpire. "That's life, kid," he'd say, "so go out there and play and don't let it get to you." An admirable philosophy.

There are other ways to cope with cheaters.

First of all, if you are playing in a tournament and are faced with a cheater, you have every right to ask for an umpire. The rules permit you to stop a match and do that.

If an umpire isn't available, or you're playing a simple match at your club or on some local court, then you have various options.

You can adapt Jack Kramer's attitude and live with it.

You can decide to play out the match and then file a protest with your club pro or the tournament officials.

In fact, on the junior and senior circuits, where an umpire is not automatically assigned to each match, word spreads quickly on cheaters. Tournament officials anticipate complaints and trouble with the labeled players and try to assign referees to every round they play. Usually, the tournament committee tells them something like, "We're sorry. We don't know if you have difficulty seeing, but we've had a substantial number of complaints about your line calls. . . ."

You might confront the cheater, but then you have to be prepared for his response as well as your own.

I have found it more effective to be polite. "You and I obviously are seeing the ball differently on your side of the court. What would you like to do about it?"

That sort of response has the benefit of signaling your opponent that while he is on notice, you are not directly accusing him of cheating. It further sucks him into the whole process: We have to solve this together, you seem to be saying. He might very well suggest you both seek a linesperson. But if none is available, I assure you that nevertheless you have stunned him. No one has ever asked him this question before and it will take some — if not a sufficient — toll on him. Meanwhile, you must face reality and do the best you can, bolstering yourself with the thought that you are playing this person for the last time.

Trying to reach cheaters on a deeper level and effecting change in them is also possible, but never easy. Some years back at a club where I was the professional, twelve members sat down with a cheater, who was very important in the club, and said: "Look, we care about you as a human being. We care about you as a club member. We feel we have to tell you that we have never seen anything like this. . . . We all feel that you're terrible on line calls. We don't know if it's your eyes, or what's happening. But as a group we want you to know how concerned we are about this."

They talked it through. It was difficult for the members to do, but it changed the man, rather quickly and quite profoundly.

One final point about cheating. As we'll see in Chapter 11,

our tests have demonstrated that no matter who is making the call, no one is capable of seeing with real accuracy. Not you, not your opponent, not the umpire. The ball is on the court only about three milliseconds, and the human eye doesn't record a three-millisecond event.

Also, when the ball looks "just out," it's probably "just in" because, even though the naked eye cannot see this happen, the ball rolls about two inches after hitting the court before it bounces off. Two inches one way or the other can change an awful lot of calls.

Toughness

You are down 4–1 in the set and you start muttering to yourself: "Get tough! . . . Dig in!"

The idea of urging yourself on might be fine, but unfortunately, when you do it that way you give your system a command that may adversely affect your muscle contractions. For most people, that pretty much means you will start to lose points.

We have tested people under these circumstances, using a little black box called a Bassin Timer to record the effects of stress on stroke production. The Bassin Timer is an electrical device that sends light down a ramp and the person being tested tries to stop the light at a given spot. We have also used electromyography, which converts electrical activity associated with active skeletal muscle into a visual record.

We found that when players decide consciously to "get tough," and try to pump themselves up, their timing often gets worse by 30 or 40 milliseconds. That's more than enough to destroy any shot.

The problem here starts with the very concept of toughness.

Being tough, whatever that means, does not have anything to do with being able to hit a ball correctly. And that's what matters in tennis, whether you are down 4–1 or up 4–1.

Execution is the name of the game, and execution has nothing to do with being tougher than your opponent or with the quality of your character suggested by that dreadful macho cliché, "When the going gets tough, the tough get going."

There are any number of books on "mental toughness." Responsible authors talk about "healthy mental toughness," by which they mean developing self-esteem, being in physical shape, practicing efficiently, scouting your opponent, focusing on important issues.

Among the most important issues are getting into position to hit the ball, addressing it properly, and hitting it in the center of your strings, none of which has anything to do with being gritty.

Imagine yourself out on the court in a close match, about to break your opponent's serve, and you are worrying about winning or losing. "Could I lose this?" you ask yourself. "I've got a 40–30 lead in this game. *I've got to get this point!*"

If you approach the moment that way, you could well be setting yourself up to lose. You are sending the brain a signal that is going to affect the way your muscles respond. As a result, your chances of losing that point normally increase, unless of course you get lucky and your opponent hands it to you.

Think how differently it would be if you were not thinking about the consequences of the next point, but rather about the shot you wanted to hit on that point, that return of your opponent's serve. Imagine how differently you would feel if you were not flooded by your determination to win.

If you can do that, you defuse the moment.

And with that, you free yourself to focus on the ball.

Especially at tough times, remember that the ball does not know how you feel, nor does it care. The ball does not know you are up a point for service break. The ball does not know what the score is, whether this is the first point of the match or the last point of the match. The ball does not know that you have lost to Phil every week for the last twenty and if you can beat him today it will make you feel absolutely wonderful, even though your business has never been worse and your teenage daughter keeps threatening to run away from home.

The ball must be hit in a particular way, a highly specific manner, regardless at what point in the match you're hitting it.

The ball, my friend, has no brain or emotions.

Playing It Safe

You might not find yourself playing Connors in the quarterfinals of the U.S. Open, but I'm sure you've found yourself in a comparable situation.

You're up in a set and the match and you can taste victory. You say, "Okay, now just don't make any mistakes. You're almost there. Just hang on and play steady."

If you do that, you have greatly increased your chances to lose. Because when you do that, you alter your style of playing, and that alters the way that your body responds.

Once again, we see that your muscles will be contracted differently from the way they had been contracted earlier.

You may go to hit a passing shot, for example. Earlier in the set, when you weren't in this mode of thinking, you hit the backhand however you thought it should be hit. You prepared for it properly, hit it down the line with nice topspin, and it worked. You hit a beautiful passing shot and won the point.

Another time you could see that your opponent was expecting you to hit down the line so you hit a nice crosscourt backhand. Maybe a gentle backhand lob. Whatever it was, you were focusing on the job that had to be done, on how you had to hit the ball at that time, and you were not thinking about playing it safe. Your brain did not receive any conflicting messages. The message was "backhand," and it responded by summoning all the right muscles.

Now, thinking about playing it safe, you hit the ball tentatively. You end up somewhere between your old software package and the new conservative one. As a result, you hit a ball that doesn't pass anything or anyone. It plops into the net.

If you get ahead in a match, never allow yourself to fall into that "if I can just hang on" attitude.

If you are tempted, remember this: You got to 5–2 playing a certain style, sending certain signals from your brain to your muscles. If you change, you change those signals.

Furthermore, you not only alter your own game, but you give your opponent a new chance at life. You change the way he was losing. When your new game doesn't work, your confidence drops while your opponent's confidence begins to rise.

A meaningful psychological shift occurs. You change from being a person in control to being a passive player who has abandoned his own game.

Now, you are not so much playing as praying.

That will not help. Instead, keep hitting the ball just the way you were hitting it. Keep sending the same messages to your brain. You are not going to win by praying. You've got to make it happen yourself.

Win Fast, Lose Fast

When I asked the woman why she was in such a rush, she was puzzled.

Like so many people who have a need to win fast or lose fast, she was unaware of how she was playing. She was unaware that something was compelling her to finish every point in three shots, that if it wasn't over at that stage, she would end it, either by bashing one against the fence or getting lucky with a winner.

Take a look at your own game. Perhaps, like that woman, you play at a similar pitch, with a similar compulsion, and are not aware of it.

Quite common is the experience of the long point. As a point stretches out, feelings begin to surface that you are not comfortable with. "I must win this point . . . I must . . . "

To dispel those feelings or the deeper issues connected with them, you stop playing each shot as best you can, and force the point: You are suddenly determined to end this nightmare; you are going to win it fast or lose it fast, but one way or the other, you are going to end this point.

Obviously, people who play that way do not have much tolerance for frustration. And that is not a very good temperament for tennis. If you encounter it in an opponent, you can dramatically increase your chance to win with perseverance. Solid patience should be your strategy. Your strokes should be high, soft, and deep. To hit hard will only feed the game and personality needs of that opponent with a low frustration threshold.

To be sure, there are people who play the win-fast-lose-fast game and are quite content with it. They tell me they get their pleasure out of hitting every ball hard. They don't expect consistency, or even very much success. I suppose if they can also expect to lose a great deal, even to people who hardly know how to play, and they are comfortable with that, then they will remain reasonably satisfied with their tennis.

Among this school, I have found what I call cathartic players. Tennis for them is a way to release stress, to release aggression. That's what they play for.

There are also people who maintain that is why they play, but when you watch them, you know something else is happening. These are the type-A executives who rave about the release they get from tennis, about the joys of "letting it all hang out." But on the court they scream at themselves and their opponents, swear over every point. In fact, they haven't left the office. The tennis court is merely a temporary change of venue, another place to act out problems and exhibit the behavior that goes with them.

Often these are the same people who announce that they don't care about the score, but the way they suffer every point they lose reveals the opposite.

Stuttering and Uncertainty

There's an interesting if controversial theory about speech stuttering that has great relevance for tennis and the mind-body connection. Called the approach-avoidance conflict, it was developed by the late Dr. Joseph Sheehan, a psychologist and specialist in speech therapy, and is especially meaningful to me, because I worked with him during some graduate studies at UCLA.

Essentially Sheehan's idea is that an individual wants to speak but simultaneously doesn't want to speak. He or she is caught in the middle and the result is stuttering. We know the brain can send only one signal to the same area at the same time. Quite separately, psychoanalytic theory runs along similar lines of ambivalence.

In tennis you find the approach-avoidance conflict all the time. You want to hit — you don't want to hit. You change your mind in the middle of shots. When that happens, you almost always miss. The shot goes halfway between one idea and the other. Try to remember, the brain can send to the muscle system only one software package at a time.

For example, you are going to hit down the line, then at the last instant decide to go crosscourt. The ball hits the bottom of the net, halfway between those two points.

Or you decide you're going to hit a certain kind of serve and you change your mind in the middle of it. You double-fault.

Or you get set to hit an overhead and then take your eye off the ball to check where your opponent is. She fakes a run to the right and you think: "Aha! Now I've got her." You end up whiffing it.

Avoid that. Make up your mind where you're going to hit the overhead and let the other person guess. If you hit the ball correctly, the odds are your opponent is probably not going to get it anyway. You'll have too much power and speed on it. But if you try to guess where that person is about to go, you've got too much to do.

You are overloading your brain circuits and putting yourself under too much stress.

A similar phenomenon occurs when a ball takes a bad bounce. Your brain makes a decision about where, when, and how to hit an approaching ball long before it has bounced. It must. If the decision is made after the bounce, there will not be enough time to recruit the muscles to hit the ball.

As noted, in most situations you need a minimum of some 200 milliseconds to recruit the muscles from the brain to the stroke. But after the ball bounces, you have less than 200 milliseconds. So when it takes a bad bounce, you are hardly ever able to return it.

While there might not be much you can do about bad bounces, you can deal with uncertainty in other forms by eliminating ambivalence, ruling out variables, and making decisions and shots automatically (which we'll explore in Chapter 13).

For example, with many shots, you can do this even before you get out on the court. Tell yourself, "All right, if he hits crosscourt to me, I'm going to hit deep crosscourt back." That's it. You've got it set and you won't get caught in the trap of setting, then changing your mind on that kind of shot.

When you precondition yourself, you are also applying another useful theory, this one from psychologist Rainer

Martens: "Learning takes place when there's an absence of uncertainty."

A fine goal: Eliminate uncertainty where you can.

Begin with a game plan. How are you going to play this person? If you decide that you are going to return forehands crosscourt, that becomes part of your plan. It doesn't matter whether your opponent figures it out, because if you hit the ball well, then she's going to be in trouble anyway.

When you approach a game or a match this way, ruling out as much uncertainty as you can, you have greatly simplified life and tennis: All you have to do then is get into position and hit the ball, put all your attention into hitting a particular shot as best you can.

Most people don't do that.

They get caught in the middle.

Cues and Anticipation

There's an important piece of strategy to be extracted from the eye-brain-muscle interaction.

I have spoken of the eye transmitting a message to the brain, data on the direction, speed, spin, and other qualities of the approaching ball, all of which data the brain processes to determine which software package the muscles require for the most effective response.

I also noted in the previous chapter that when Helen hit her dinky slice forehand to you, the very motion of her arm provided an important piece of data, a cue, which enabled your brain to prepare for the shot, to anticipate it even before it left her racket.

All of that happens without your making any conscious effort. But in fact, you can train yourself to pick up cues. Your pro can work with you on it. Then you can make a conscious effort at it, and if you do, cues and anticipation can improve enormously the way you play.

A few years ago, I worked with a group of specialists in

hand-eye coordination in a study of a number of leading pros, and to my amazement, one of the great champions of the game ranked lowest in that important category. However, he was first by far when we tested anticipation of shots.

From a considerable amount of testing with intermediate-level players that we've done at the Tennis College, it is clear that they get their cues for hitting the ball very early. Before the ball has bounced, nearly all of the cues about the nature of that ball have already been signaled to the brain and the brain has encoded everything.

I often asked them to close their eyes as the ball bounced in front of them, then try to hit it. To their surprise, they hit perfectly good forehands and backhands.

The same anticipatory cuing process occurs in baseball. I hate to make baseball fans weep, but for years it was reported that Ted Williams could see the ball rotate and he could see the ball hit his bat. Indeed, everyone agreed, Ted Williams had super vision. But the day finally came when Ted Williams declared what sports science has shown — that it was impossible for him to have seen the ball actually hit the bat. In fact, neither Ted nor any human being had ever seen the ball hit the bat. It is on the bat from one to three milliseconds.

Rod Carew, another great baseball hitter, told me that the best hitters make their decision to hit the ball before it is actually released from the pitcher's hand. "What you are really doing," he said, "is taking your cues off the body movements of the pitcher."

That made a lot of sense to me because research clearly shows that given the rate a normal fastball travels, if a batter makes his decision after the ball is eighteen feet out of the pitcher's hand — or about a third of the way to home plate — it will be too late to hit most pitches. He will strike out.

Apply this to your tennis game. The better you get at picking up cues from your opponent's body, the more you can anticipate shots. And anticipation will get you to the ball faster, and improve your game in a number of ways.

In addition to working with your instructor to hone this skill, there is a technique you can teach yourself: Pull up a chair and watch the C or B player you've always wanted to beat. You'd be amazed at what you can learn from the sidelines. (So often tennis players don't start using their tennis brains until they have their hand on the grip of the racket.)

As you watch, start guessing. From what you see, is she going to go down the line, or is she going to go crosscourt? Imagine yourself being the other player. Is she going to hit to your forehand, or to your backhand?

Begin to call the shots: I think she's going down the line. Nah, she goes crosscourt. Now you think she's going crosscourt, and she does go crosscourt.

You can even keep score for yourself with this drill and see how many you guess right. But more important is staying with the exercise. Because for the first time you are starting to pay attention to that player's cues.

As you do this, your brain will begin to register your future opponent's signature on particular strokes. From that, you can develop a mental model to simplify the process. For example, register the cues that announce that she's going crosscourt. If she doesn't show you those cues, you know she's going down the line.

When she goes crosscourt, perhaps she pulls her shoulder. She turns her foot. She places the hand that's off the racket in a certain position. That's her signature. You start to observe those characteristics and log them in your brain. Once that information is in place, when you see it on the court, you will know where she is going to hit the ball. And if you know where an opponent is going to hit the ball, you can beat almost anybody in the world because you can practically walk for a volley.

That is how good professional players respond to opponents. It is how you want to respond to your opponents. When you get that first cue, respond to it.

To do this, you must not only learn to anticipate, but also be prepared to anticipate wrongly. Part of this is experiencing what I call the "joy of running the wrong way." When you're practicing anticipation, you've got to be free to make a mistake. If you have a conservative nature, you'll wait until you see the ball go and only then will you move. As you undoubtedly realize, you're going to be too late.

In fact, many people know where the ball is going, but they don't trust themselves.

With a special camera called the Eye Mark Recorder, I have tracked the eyes of students. With some, their pupils followed the ball all right, but the students didn't respond with their feet, only their eyes.

To counter this, I started to give them permission to run the wrong way. We set up a drill in which I would not tell them where I would hit, but encourage them to take a guess.

Then I would say, "Okay, now this time I want you to guess, and we'll reward you for being wrong as well as for being right. The reward is simply for going."

Amazingly, these students not only improved dramatically, they were stunned to find out how much court they could cover, if they trusted themselves and started early.

The top players are never afraid to commit themselves. Of course, every once in a while they do run the wrong way. They move toward the line, anticipating a shot on the backhand; instead their opponent goes crosscourt and they do look a bit silly to the average fan.

Nevertheless, the pro is not afraid to take a cue and go with it. I was struck how Stefan Edberg guessed right or anticipated on several critical points against Michael Chang and Pete Sampras in the 1992 U.S. Open.

The more you can do that, the better you will get at it because you will soon begin to look for — and to discover — cues. Before long, your guesses will become quite educated, because as noted, there are patterns and the brain can log them, if you are looking for them.

As you develop your instincts and facilities for anticipating, you will find that you are making more and more correct calls and, consequently, moving yourself more and more frequently into the right position. That, of course, enables you to prepare properly for your shots, which will produce meaningful results.

Watching the pros, you might not notice, but they are continually working to arrive at the right spot early so they have plenty of time to hit as they want. Today, the best players even study computer printouts that track how and where their toughest opponents are likely to hit under particular conditions.

Anticipating correctly also gives you a special feeling of pleasure, the feeling that you really are playing smart tennis. You are taking charge, gaining a special and delicious advantage.

Try playing a match where you do nothing but start running before the ball is hit. It is a remarkable drill.

All you are concerned about in this match is anticipating. You become completely focused on picking up the cues from your opponent's body, responding and moving on the basis of those cues. As you'll discover, there is enormous satisfaction in getting to a spot early against a hard hitter, as opposed to being forced into one defensive measure after another, or being forced into stretching for your life simply to return the ball.

Let me mention one other kind of wacko anticipation drill I've tried with wonderful results. It's especially useful when you're down in a match.

Your opponent hits you a backhand. You turn and run the other way. Go to the forehand corner and take a perfect swing. Watch what happens to your opponent. He'll stand there staring at you and you'll win five games in a row. It takes an opponent a long time to recover from such a shocking sight. They've never seen anybody run the wrong way and take a perfect swing.

/ CHAPTER 4

Dumping Psychological Baggage

PEOPLE BRING lots of psychological baggage with them onto the tennis court.

There are fears and there are anxieties. There are full-blown neuroses.

I have seen these problems operating at all levels of the game. A fear of failure, for example, kept one of my pupils, an accomplished surgeon, from learning. A need to lose kept another extremely good player from hardly ever winning. One quite successful pro had a tendency to punish himself, and given half a chance, he would do so by dropping a match.

Obviously, some of these problems run deeper than others. Some, like the fear of failure, could be worked out simply through a conversation between the surgeon and myself. Others, if they were to be understood, would require extended therapy.

No book is going to rid you of a complicated neurosis. But we can look at some of the problems you might be able to cope with yourself, if you can recognize them; as well as others for which you might indeed want to get help.

The CBS Complex

First, some general principles, psychologically sound for tennis and not bad for the rest of life as well:

- Try to be honest with yourself.
- Try to be selfish in a healthy way, to play for yourself, blocking from your mind concerns of what others might think of you. After all, you have no power over what people think of you.
- Try to be realistic about your goals and your limitations. Otherwise, you run the risk of continually frustrating yourself. This might mean admitting that you are not a graceful, blond Nordic god like Stefan Edberg. That you are not a powerful, sultry Latin goddess like Gabriela Sabatini. If you are ten years older and ten pounds heavier than you would like to be in your ideal self-image, you will enjoy the game infinitely more if you factor those realities into your expectations.
- Try not to play as if you were on center court, Wimbledon, on CBS. Playing under those conditions can impose a bit of extra pressure on your shaky second serve and generally be a touch distracting. I assure you that you will play better, if you give yourself a chance to concentrate on your strokes. To avoid putting yourself under such pressure, you might ask yourself this question: When was the last time CBS called you for the results of your weekly match with George or Helen?

Fear of Failure

In the opening session of a program at my Tennis College, I tell everyone that they have come to a mistake center.

Accept an important gift, I urge them: While you are

learning, you have total impunity. You are free to make every possible mistake imaginable. Hit the ball over the fence. Swing and miss completely. Fall over your own feet.

This is where you come to make mistakes. And then discover their causes and cures.

This is what learning motor skills is all about, I explain. No one learns a motor skill without a struggle. If you can accept that and appreciate it, you have gone a long way in the learning process. The struggle, in fact, is the key to learning, and without it, there is none.

Each time you make a mistake, figure it out, and, with a certain amount of real effort, cure it, you automatically reward yourself. You will know and feel the pleasure of progress and achievement. You are going to feel very good about yourself.

I tell them this for terribly important psychological reasons. I know that learning tennis can be a slow, difficult, frustrating process, one that injures self-esteem, one that can trigger any number of anxieties.

Some people cannot learn a new sport or develop a new skill without surfacing the anxieties of childhood, when for example the loss of parental love seemed to be riding on how quickly and how well they excelled in the classroom and on the athletic field. They are adults now, but those anxieties can still grip them, and they won't understand why. They won't know why they are unable to relax and give this new sport a chance. They won't be able to say to themselves, "I've hardly ever played tennis. I can't expect very much of myself. No one can. But let me give it a fling."

I'm trying to head off such anxieties. I'm trying to give them the right to play crummy.

Sometimes I succeed; sometimes I don't.

I recall one overachiever, an interesting man who was president of a large international investment company. He came to the college and the first day in my introductory talk I told him and all the others in his class that they thought they had signed up for a tennis college but in truth they had enrolled in a mistake center.

During that first day, I saw him, performing awkwardly but making progress, the kind of development I might hope for with a middle-aged beginner who was in reasonable shape, fairly well coordinated, and not overly troubled about looking foolish.

That night, my wife, Melody, and I went to a restaurant in a town near Coto de Caza. The man I'm speaking of came over as we entered and asked us if we would like to join him for dinner. (That happens frequently with students.) We did, and I asked him what he did for a living.

He told me and immediately added: "You know, I have lived in mortal fear of coming here."

"Why?"

"Because all my vice-presidents play tennis, and I don't. I do a lot of other things, most of them better than they do, but I don't play tennis, never had the opportunity to learn, and I'll tell you that I was terrified of looking bad. I don't like to look bad at anything, to be honest with you, and the whole idea of learning and looking bad just filled me with awful fear. But, today, I've got to thank you. From the very beginning, you made me feel so comfortable. I cannot tell you what a load you've taken off my shoulders."

It was something to hear. A man who had accomplished as much as he had, but was afraid to step out on a tennis court and make mistakes or look awkward.

Another time, I remember giving a lesson to a man who was doing something I'd never ever seen before. He was missing balls completely. Now and then he'd bounce one off the frame of his racket, but otherwise, nothing — complete whiffs, one after another.

I began to think that perhaps he suffered from some neurological impairment.

So after a while, I walked up to the net and beckoned

him forward. "What do you do for a living?" I asked him.

"I'm a brain surgeon," he said.

Wow, I thought, this guy's liable to take out a kneecap. Clearly, we needed to explore this further with what I call "a lesson intervention." So I explained to him that I thought I could do more for him if I knew more about him, and asked if he'd mind a brief discussion.

"Fine," he said.

We went into my small office and I asked him some general questions about his background and it turned out he had gotten the highest score ever in his medical school. In fact, with everything he had ever done in life, he was number one. Now he was in his forties and starting out with tennis. He had been so involved with his work, he simply hadn't found time to start earlier.

While we were talking, he took several little golf pencils out of a box on my desk and began to arrange them in intricate patterns. I couldn't take my eyes off his fingers. He was making the most delicate designs, all the while talking to me, yet the tips of the pencils never touched, and all the while he answered all my questions, never losing a thread of our conversation.

Did he feel he had the right to be lousy at anything? I asked him.

"Lousy?" he said. "Well, no, to be honest with you, I really don't. You know everything has always come pretty easy for me," he continued, whipping those pencils around.

"That may be," I told him, "but I think we have a special problem here, one that you as a doctor will readily appreciate. Tennis is a game involving both small- and large-muscle skills," I explained, "and learning large-muscle physical skills is quite different from learning academic skills and small-muscle movements, both of which you have obviously mastered, given your great success as a surgeon and the remarkable way you can manipulate those little pencils."

He paused in his designing, looked up at me, and smiled.

"Which simply means," I continued, "tennis is not going to be so easy. Though I have no reason to think you can't become good at it. Meanwhile, feel free to make mistakes."

He said nothing.

"Let me add one thought. I deeply believe that anything worth doing is worth doing lousy at least once," I told him, a piece of advice I'd picked up from Dr. Jordan Paul, a psychologist. "And, even though we try to teach people in our society that making mistakes is terrible, the truth is that making mistakes is beautiful because that's how you learn."

He looked at me for a moment, then nodded slowly, smiling a bit. "I've never thought of that," he said.

We went back on the court and once again I was flabbergasted. He stopped missing every ball and he began to hit. He was not ready for the U.S. Open, mind you, but he was a completely different player out there, hitting the ball nicely.

I knew that he had stopped trying so hard not to look bad. Before, he had been straining so to be perfect, he could not possibly recruit the muscles he needed to hit the ball at all. He was so anxiety-ridden, analyzing every possible element, so scared of making any mistake, he was totally disoriented. At times he didn't look as if he knew where he was, or where the ball was.

But now, he was able to say to himself: "Hey, it's okay that I cannot do something. It's okay that I am not perfect at this."

At the Ski College, we've found that people equate falling in the snow with failure. But the truth is that you can't learn to ski without making some falls. And for beginners, those who fall the most trying new things usually make the greatest gains.

With skiing, tennis, whatever you're learning, you don't know what you're doing right until you understand what you were doing wrong. In fact, in Ski College, once we got that idea across — and implicit in it is that you are going to take a certain number of falls while learning — the greater gains we saw. If people were trying not to fall in order to preserve some image of themselves, then they wouldn't try to carve that turn, or work on getting that edge the way it should be on the turn, and they would never discover what the right way *feels* like.

They were unwilling to commit to the risk to learn. That's what learning requires — a risk. I have found that the more I and my staff are able to show beginners, in skiing and tennis, that we care about them, the more they are willing to take the risk to learn. Inevitably, once they do, they discover such wonderful new sensations that their willingness to risk increases, and of course so does their learning.

Unfortunately, in our society, everything that happens in sports — and for the most part in the rest of life as well — rewards you for not making mistakes. Just listen to football coaches and fans scream at kids when they drop a pass.

This same problem can keep D and C tennis players from ever improving. They are afraid to experiment. They are afraid to make errors. They are afraid of looking foolish.

The problem is compounded if they are unfortunate enough to be learning in a class with instructors who are not very nurturing and supportive. We all need to be nurtured when we're starting — tennis, or anything new.

It certainly applies to the learning and educational process for children. I taught school and shared the educational process with children at the elementary level for three years, at the university level another three, and worked with children as a school psychologist for two more. Scream at and punish them for mistakes, and they don't learn. Support them, guide them, show patience, and above all help them feel completely comfortable about making mistakes, about learning and you change their world. Give them an environment in which they can focus on the learning, in which they can be sufficiently relaxed to be engaged by a subject, get excited about, say, reading, rather than continually stressed over whether they are reading fast enough or not, give them that supportive and nurturing environment, and you will have children who feel good about themselves, who as a result start to learn better, who grow up loving school and all it represents. You will have children with the capacity for pleasure in their learning.

When I first started to teach, I remember watching children in the class when we read aloud. Many were not listening, but rather were frantically reading ahead so that when their turn came to read aloud, they wouldn't look stupid. I could understand that, certainly, but I knew that by responding to their anxieties and fears in that way, they would not grasp the meaning of the book — they would simply be getting the words right. And they certainly wouldn't get any joy from their reading.

So I asked all the children to put their books down and just listen. "Enjoy what's being read, and don't worry about getting the words right when your turn comes," I told them. "It's the first time you're reading this stuff. You'll make mistakes. Don't worry about it."

The capacity for pleasure in learning is one of life's great gifts. I tried to make it available to children I taught years ago, and I try to make it available now to adults, who, after all, when they come to the Tennis College are rather like children trying to learn a new subject. What I have seen over the years is that given a supportive environment when learning, children and adults alike can make enormous breakthroughs and feel enormous joy.

Net Phobia

You can have fun in tennis if you don't go to the net, but after you reach a certain level, you won't grow much as a player without playing net.

Also, without going to the net, you're depriving yourself of some of the greatest thrills and pleasures in the game.

I've lost track of the number of students who were afraid of the net, didn't know how to play it, didn't even want to learn. And they all had good excuses, usually something like: "I've got to get my ground strokes down first." Even Monica Seles confessed recently: "I keep finding excuses why I shouldn't go to the net."

Nevertheless, once I get students to try going to the net and teach them what to do there, they are astonished at how much it improves their tennis and increases their fun.

Indeed, once you get a taste, it can be addictive. Eight or nine years ago at the tennis college we had a woman who ran to the net and froze. I asked her why and she said, "Because the ball is going to hit me." And it did. People bounced balls off her body the whole week she was there.

"Why don't you back up?" I suggested to her, thinking that perhaps if she could accept the idea that by backing up she would have a bit more time to hit the ball, she'd defrost.

"When I back up," she replied, "I just seem to get hit a little farther back."

"Then why go to the net?" I asked.

And she answered: "Because I love to attack."

The thrills are there, yet resistance is widespread, even though playing at the net is easier in many ways. True, some shots can be tough — say, volleying a return of serve that is sinking rapidly toward your feet. And, lest we forget, staying back on the baseline saves your having to run up. Tennis players, being human, can be lazy.

But look at the advantages. Often you don't need to execute with the demanding precision of a ground stroke from the baseline. Usually, you don't have to provide much power, either, since it's provided by your opponent.

Even if you mishit a shot at the net, your chances of winning the point are extremely high. If you are up close to the net, you might be able to hit within a field of 130–140 degrees, whereas if you are at the baseline, your hitting area narrows to 19.1 degrees.

Further, you can win a point at the net quickly, and save energy.

All of which, in a completely rational world, should make playing at the net relatively stress-free. But of course it doesn't. Many people are so terrified of playing at the net that they scream when you put them up there and hit practice balls at them.

The angst frequently stems from the knowledge that at the net you do need good reflexes. The ball normally comes with some speed and people think they can't respond quickly enough.

Some people have a fear of getting hit by the ball, although you hardly endanger your limbs or life if you do get hit. (An exception is being struck in the eye. That can be serious, and I normally recommend protective goggles. Sooner or later, someone will create designer goggles and then, of course, everyone will wear them.)

But otherwise, even if Boris Becker bashed you with his meanest forehand (though that is unlikely for most readers of this book) and it caught you smack on the shoulder, all you would suffer is a sting to the shoulder, comparable to a sudden slap on the back. I have seen players turn their back to an opponent's overhead — a wise and protective move — have it hit them on the shoulder and bounce into the stands, and walk away with nothing more than a red bruise.

Still, the fear remains. Underlying all the resistance is once again, I think, that pervasive fear of looking stupid. People worry they won't have the reflexes to respond to a speeding ball, that they won't be able to move quickly enough to hit it, or they won't be able to do more than hit it on the frame of the racket and end up looking like an awkward clown.

In fact, when you first start to play at the net, I can guarantee that you will feel and look awkward. How can it be otherwise? Everything will be new, your movements will not be smooth, and you won't be able to anticipate shots very well, so you will have to make sudden changes. It will take time for you to adjust and create the new software you need.

Meanwhile, I recommend two ways to deal with this new assault on your self-esteem:

First, this is a time to be totally selfish. Don't give a hoot how you look to anybody else.

And, second, you might try a larger racket, a 110, unless you find that a larger racket gives you trouble on your serve, as it does for some people. The bigger face will give you that much more of a chance to get your racket on the ball at the net. Also, the new racket provides more power on off-center hits.

A larger racket might also provide you with another, unexpected advantage.

In one of the early studies we did when the new oversized racket came on the market, our most significant finding was that players who used it moved their feet faster while volleying at the net.

Since they were no longer afraid of being hit by the ball — they felt the oversized racket gave them that much more protection — they felt safe. They could remove a deep anxiety that at the net they would lose control over the game and themselves.

With all that gone, they had no further need to cower and shrink. They could be free with themselves and their bodies, they could aggressively move their feet, they could, as that wonderful frozen woman would say, really attack the ball.

The Fear of Winning

Winning affects us in unexpected ways.

Basically, it seems to me, healthy people do like to win. They don't like to win no matter how they win or no matter what price they have to pay to win. They don't like to win above everything else, above a good learning experience, for example. But they enjoy winning.

At the same time, it is clear that some people have problems with winning. I've seen people who have unbelievable talent and yet they never win. And when I encounter that, it leads me to suspect that it must be in their best interest — or what they *think* is their best interest — to lose. They must be getting some rewards from losing.

Let's take the example of a player who needs a great deal of attention. He or she is just a social player, and certainly could win, say, two matches out of ten. But, in fact, that player gets a lot more attention losing ten matches out of ten than losing only eight out of ten.

By losing, he's very successful at what he's trying to do — which is not to play good tennis. What he's really trying to do is get attention.

And, he's also trying to put himself down.

There are other losers who fit the psychological description "intra-punitive," people who masochistically injure and punish themselves.

I see a lot of people who do this by losing matches. For one reason or another, which they are not aware of, they don't like themselves. They are angry with themselves. They don't feel worthy of winning. And so rather than playing as well as they can and rewarding themselves with a victory, they deny themselves that pleasure.

I remember an interesting example of this with the pros. In the 1960s and early 1970s, when I was involved in the management of professional tournaments, I would constantly see messages from countless players posted on bulletin boards at tournaments, for one particular fellow. He was a man who was so good in practice that no one could ever beat him — in a practice match, that is. So, everybody wanted to play him because they knew that he would sharpen their game before the tournament. However, he never got beyond the first round in tournament play.

Naturally, I always wondered: If he could beat their brains out all the time in practice when there was no pressure, what did that say? Too obviously, that he could not handle the pressure of a tournament.

But there was something else here. I think that this player could not handle winning. If he could beat all these other pros in practice, surely he could beat some of them in tournaments. But he had his own reasons, I'm convinced, for losing, for denying himself the satisfaction of winning.

Ken Rosewall told me about one famous pro who was quite successful, yet still suffered something of this intra-punitive problem, and the other players were aware of it.

Now, professional tennis players don't go around whispering to each other, "Joe Blow's intra-punitive." But what Ken and the others knew was that if you gave this fellow half a chance to lose a match, he'd take it.

For example, if he was playing well, and perhaps got a bad line call against him, his opponent would sympathize with him as they changed sides: "God, I mean you are getting robbed over and over."

Players threw that bait out and he would almost always bite. The effect was to drive home that, indeed, he was being robbed and it gave him an excuse for losing. In the end, if he lost the match he could console himself with the rationalization that the calls were against him.

There are also players who create a terrible anxiety of expectation: that if they win, people will expect them to win more and more. So if they do win a match, the pressure mounts until it becomes overwhelming. With this kind of problem, we see players who are capable of great upsets, but who, when they are expected to win, fall apart.

Other people have trouble winning because they fear that if they do, their opponent is not going to like them, or worse. They personalize the match in such a way that it's no longer just a tennis match.

People who have an overwhelming need to be liked or

loved by an opponent do not suddenly awaken to it in the middle of the third set. They do not suddenly say, "Hey, what I really want is for this guy to think well of me, to be my pal, to be friendly with me around the club. I'd better blow this third set." No, it's an unconscious desire. But the effect of it is the same as if they had intentionally decided to blow the third set. Unconsciously, they are not taking the risk of incurring the wrath of their opponent.

Impeccable Losers

Then there are the "impeccable losers."

These are people who look marvelous when you see them play. Great form. Great style. They dress wonderfully. Sensual. They always seem to be in position. They look like winners. They've got everything going for them . . . except putting the ball in the right place at the right time. They always lose.

People are continually saying to them, "I don't know how you could have lost that match. You looked so great out there." Remarks like that are what impeccable losers are searching for, what their reward systems need.

I remember one typical impeccable loser, a man about forty. He was tall, blond, California handsome, from a good family, had a certain amount of money, a lot of style.

I knew him and his family somewhat, and interestingly, off the tennis court, he was also an impeccable loser. He had so many attributes and assets and yet he couldn't seem to put them all together. At one point he was a stockbroker and then he was in the real estate business. Then he was a financial planner. Then he was a banker. He was all of these and none of these. A very good-looking guy, what used to be called a lady's man, he had two sad marriages that I knew of.

When you saw him out on the tennis court, you thought at first, given his smoothness, his style, his gracefulness, that he was some combination of movie star and tennis pro. But out on the court, just as in his life, he could never seem to put it all together.

He did win a certain number of matches, the result of a lifetime of instruction and playing. He had a big serve and when that was on he could usually do pretty well. But he would never do nearly as well as one might expect.

Everybody in his club knew that in order to beat him, all you had to do was play steadily and he would always beat himself.

What is distinctive and, to me, especially sad about impeccable losers is that they have so much apparent talent. If they were able to overcome their need to lose, they could be handsome winners. Sadly, I think that they are denying themselves the experience and the joy of winning, or even the profound pleasure of trying their best to win.

They set themselves up perfectly for losses, playing the martyr, or the masochistic role. They want, among other things, the attention they get for losing, and the love they feel from that attention. And they get a lot of it. As I said, people are always telling them they looked so great, they simply couldn't have lost. Of course, in their minds, when they lose, they're ahead.

There's a different kind of winning problem: often people need permission to beat other people, especially to beat them badly.

Running pro tours, I have seen variations of this. I recall one woman helping another, working with her on her game, acting as a self-appointed coach. She certainly helped the other player, but when it came to matches, her student could almost never beat her. How could you beat somebody who's trying to help you that way?

You might find yourself in a comparable situation, playing a friend or neighbor. You're up 5–love, but instead of being able to continue playing at the level that brought you to that score, you say, "C'mon, this is my friend. I can't do this to him." The next thing you know, meaning to be humane and charitable, you ease up and, in essence, give your friend three games. So now you're up 5–3 and you say to yourself, "Okay, now I'll pour it on." But you cannot.

I have heard that Michael Chang used to have great difficulty beating his brother. His brother could play tennis, was a college player. But Michael Chang was ranked hundreds of notches ahead of his brother at the time.

Give Yourself the License to Win

Jennifer Capriati has spoken interestingly of how her attitude toward winning seemed to change.

At first, her intention was to play as well as she could, but she did not think she could beat the best women. It wasn't expected of her, anyway, she knew, which probably made it easier for her to limit her goals.

However, the more she played against the best women, the more she realized, "Hey, they're not so much better than me." And with that insight, her attitude toward herself and her opponents changed. She no longer saw herself as this kid who was lucky to be allowed on the same court with the best pros. She saw herself as a legitimate rival, a contender. From then on, she said, she was not satisfied with merely playing well. She was out to beat them all.

When she beat Navratilova at Wimbledon in 1991, she spoke of beating "the lege" (as in legend). There was a touch of awe as she spoke of that achievement. But there was something else. She was not an adoring kid talking about how lucky she was to beat such an exalted champion. She was a determined professional player, still only fifteen to be sure, but clearly not thinking of herself as a child who must respect her adults. She was a tough competitor. On the court, age was immaterial to her. She was going to beat every opponent she could. This was what professional tennis was all about.

Capriati was growing up and, as part of the process of adolescence, allowing herself to think thoughts that previously she censored. It was okay, she was telling herself, to beat anybody, including famous adults. She had broken a psychological barrier and in so doing had expanded hugely her possibilities for winning.

I saw a dramatic variation of this unfold one night in St. Louis in the middle of a Davis Cup Match, the United States against Sweden in 1982.

Mats Wilander was playing John McEnroe. Before the match, Wilander made an extraordinary statement to me in an interview. "I don't have a chance," he said to me and a million viewers. "I just hope I can play well."

I was stunned and wondered for a moment if he was setting me up. I speculated on the way the Swedes at that time all seemed to be taught self-effacement and modesty right along with their two-handed backhands.

But the sincerity of his manner denied my skepticism. I was left feeling that Wilander was so convinced of his limitations, he was speaking from his heart.

McEnroe, who did regularly beat Wilander, won the first two sets, but they were close. Almost in spite of himself, Wilander was playing well. And then in the middle of the third set, I saw it happen.

Wilander won a point at the net and stared for a moment at McEnroe. Then, very slowly, he started to walk back for the next point, but he clearly was engaged in an inner dialogue. He walked to the baseline, then turned and walked in again toward the net. Then, as if returning to the court, discovering where he actually was, he walked slowly again to the baseline.

I cannot read minds, yet intuitively I thought this was the

moment when Wilander realized that he could win, when he discovered that up to then he had been trying merely to play well, not to win. But now he had changed his mind and his attitude toward the match. He was permitting himself the possibility that he could beat John McEnroe.

With some excitement, I said: "This is going to be a whale of a match." And they practically turned off my mike in the ESPN booth. They thought I must be drunk to blurt out a statement like that with Wilander down two sets. Off-air, I assured them they should be prepared for a long match: Wilander had just discovered that he could play.

Sure enough, the match went six hours and 32 minutes. Wilander took the next two sets and came within a point of winning the match. McEnroe did, finally — 9–7, 6–2, 15–17, 3–6, 8–6 — but that match was a turning point in Wilander's career. He went on to win the Australian and U.S. titles and added another French championship to his record.

A self-discovery like that is tremendously exciting. Try to give it to yourself. You can still be realistic. You are not going to beat John McEnroe, even today. But there are undoubtedly any number of other players against whom you rule out the possibility of winning. Suspend that judgment, if you can, and play the match. Give yourself the license to win. You might discover that you are better than, for whatever reasons, you gave yourself credit for being.

/ PART II

Terrific and Healthy Goals

CHAPTER 5

Know What You Want from Tennis

SOME YEARS AGO, Jan Harless, one of my staff, interviewed students at our Tennis College to find out why they played. It was part of her graduate thesis in psychology and it paralleled work I was doing at the time on why people play, and why some people want to coach.

Many of the responses she collected were fairly predictable. A lot of people, for example, told her that tennis was a fun way to exercise. On the right day, you could not only work over your body, but tan it as well. For many, it was also a way to meet people. For some, tennis was an agreeable form of competition. Others liked playing, even though they did not consider themselves competitive. Many enjoyed a sport that combined physical skill and strategy, a sport where you hit shots in conjunction with a plan.

But there were also interesting surprises in her research. To begin with, after interviewing more than 500 people, she produced over 110 different answers.

Mostly, it was clear that an awful lot of people were playing for reasons of self-esteem. Some did not feel good about their bodies, and for them tennis was a route to become trimmer and more attractive.

Nothing wrong with that, certainly, but I wondered how

many of those folks had any idea of how such attitudes could affect their playing?

If they were worried about how they looked in their tennis shorts, those skimpy things that exposed their flabby thighs, they might have difficulty concentrating on their shots. If they were trying not to look bad out on the court, they would not be very free to make mistakes, which, as we saw in the previous chapter, is essential to growth.

In my view, it won't take long before many such people abandon the game in frustration. They won't understand why, but they won't be able to hit the ball with any consistency. "This game simply isn't for me," they'll say. "Oh, well, I can still wear the nice warm-up clothes."

To some degree, I think that's what happened in the late '70s and early '80s when we had a so-called tennis boom. There were an estimated 38 million players in America. They spent small fortunes for pastel outfits and warm-up jackets and rackets in new shapes, made of space-age materials.

All was well until they got out on the court. Then, quickly, their self-images were badly violated. These people weren't willing or able to approach the game in a way that would allow them to truly learn. So, today we have more like 18 million players. (Though judging from the number of people I see in supermarkets and airports wearing tennis clothes, the other 20 million still have their wardrobes.)

Those people never gave themselves a chance to play. Their reasons for wanting to play got in the way.

The same is true for a number of others in the survey who replied that they wanted to be able to keep up with their husbands or wives. What they seemed to be saying was that if they didn't learn tennis and play well enough, they wouldn't be loved. But that places a tremendous burden on their learning and could block them from approaching the sport with a productive attitude.

As I tell my students, a reasonably healthy adult ought to be able to say: "I'm a beginner. I've hardly ever played this game before and I'm discovering it's not so easy. I don't look very graceful and I hit every other backhand into the net. But, so what? That's part of learning a new sport. And learning tennis or any sport is, let's face it, a struggle. Beyond which, what can anyone expect from a beginner? If people, and that includes my husband/wife, can't accept me for being a D player, that's really their problem, not mine."

That's the frame of mind I urge people at the Tennis College to develop. It's very different from playing out of the fear of loss of love, an infantile fear that can be paralyzing.

It is much closer to another attitude I have mentioned, that of healthy selfishness, of playing for yourself and your own satisfactions first.

But I think you can begin to see, as I did with the results of that survey, that your reasons for playing are important and possibly complicated.

Furthermore, knowing what you are looking for from tennis will affect everything you do with the sport, from how much you play to how much you practice to your attitude on the court.

Goals and Reality

When it comes to establishing goals that are realistic, I find the greatest problems with parents (more in Chapter 7). The famous tennis parent, like a stage parent, projects the most fantastical ambitions onto a poor child, and then mauls the child for not measuring up.

I urge adults who come to the Tennis College to be honest with themselves, which after all is a fundamental principle of mental health. If they have difficulties doing that with their tennis skills and goals, I suggest they ask friends with whom they play to evaluate their games honestly.

To be sure, I don't have a lot of adults come to the Tennis College declaring that they intend to reach the finals in the U.S. Open. But I do find many with unrealistic expectations of themselves, and that leads to great fits and self-flagellation when they miss shots and lose games. The truth is they don't have the shots they imagine they do.

"Truths may be painful," Robert Firestone and Joyce Catlett observe in their book, *The Truth*. "They may destroy illusions you have about yourself and your life. But facing the truth is the only way to live your life fully," a piece of wisdom echoed by great psychologists from Shakespeare through Freud.

Establishing realistic goals will give you a nice sense of direction. It can inform the way you practice and the way you play.

Once you can admit to your limitations and problems, then you can focus on and attack each stroke you need.

Back in Chapter 2, we saw how you developed the approach shot you so badly needed, and how that expanded your entire game, adding a net game to your tactics. Next you might face weaknesses with your second serve and return of serve, two of the most important points in the game that are also two of the most overlooked. You might then spend practice sessions doing nothing but hitting that second serve to Alice and returning her practice serves as well. Then play a match where every serve is hit like a second serve, and your greatest concentration goes to return of serve.

Do that, follow realistic goals, and you will improve.

Improve, and you will feel better about yourself.

Assess Yourself Mentally

There are a number of personality characteristics that affect the way you play tennis, and to some degree they can determine your level of play. It's worth looking at these in relation to your own personality. You might see reasons why you find it hard to improve, and note aspects of your own personality that bear watching. You might also be able to measure your possibilities for development.

Curiosity

You need to be asking yourself what's keeping you back. What are the holes in your game? Do you play defensively too much of the time? Why don't you want to go to the net? Why do you lose? Why do you win? Are you being truthful in evaluating your own game?

Some people ask themselves these essential questions automatically. They are continually analyzing their games and themselves. Others approach tennis in a rather mindless fashion, playing against the same opponents every week, committing the same errors, achieving the same results. Even playing on the same court. That sort of mechanical approach locks you onto a plateau, a fixed level of playing, in which you are using the same old comfortable software packages, whether they are effective or not. For most people, that soon leads to frustration and boredom.

If you find that happening to you, make an effort to change. Stop going through the motions. Make a conscious effort to think about your playing, to analyze what you are doing, what you need to be doing out on the court. And, what you are feeling.

Perseverance

Tennis is a slow-growth sport.

I know that is not the kind of news you hear much at tennis camps where you get the feeling that in a week you will practically be ready for the pro tour.

We all like instant gratification. But for tennis you need the kind of personality that can tolerate frustration and will stay with a project. It also greatly helps, as we'll see in the next chapter, if you have the kind of instructor who can make you feel comfortable while you're feeling uncomfortable, who can provide support along with advice.

This is not to say that everything between the first ball you miss completely and a comfortable B-level full-court game need be agony. To the contrary. Every step of the way, you will see improvement and, from that, experience great pleasure. During this uncomfortable time, if you understand and enjoy the learning process and the sense of growth it brings, you will feel tremendous gratification. But it won't be immediate and it will be mixed with frustration. Which is not so different, after all, from so many other worthwhile pursuits in life.

Perfectionism

There are people who must master an undertaking quickly, or they want nothing to do with it. But tennis takes time. I've never seen anyone who was good at it immediately.

These same perfectionists cannot enjoy the process of improvement, or find pleasure at various stages of development. They must be very good, or the sport is empty.

I've encountered any number of adults like this who are just starting. With some, like the surgeon-beginner, I can make a difference by talking with them. With others, however, tennis is simply not their sport.

Control

Another problem trait: People who must be in control of everyone and everything around them are going to find tennis difficult.

There are too many variables. You cannot control the infinite variety and quality of shots coming from your opponent, or the shifting sun, wind, and natural elements. Nor can you control your opponent's behavior. He gets mad about hitting a backhand wide and starts cursing and banging his racket on the court. The control freak, as I have witnessed so many times, is first puzzled by that response, since he himself would behave quite differently. Then, he is disturbed by it. But there is nothing he can do. He cannot control his opponent's responses, and if the match matters at all to him, he is soon disturbed himself.

Flexibility

In tennis, rather than being controlling, you're much better off if you can be flexible.

Each day, each match you are playing against a different kind of player, a different style, perhaps on a different court surface, and you have to adjust.

We see this very clearly with the pros. Connors was best on a hard surface, McEnroe enjoyed great success on grass, but both were substantially weaker on clay. Lendl, however, was very strong on clay but had considerable difficulty adapting to grass.

Steffi Graf has spoken of her problems of going to the net, yet she breezed through the 1992 Wimbledon final, but lost in the quarter-finals in the 1992 U.S. Open. She can adjust and rise to special challenges, but she still has difficulty being flexible enough to do that on a consistent basis.

A few years ago, her coach said that Steffi's reply to such criticism was, "Why change? I'm number one in the world." Perhaps, except that she has now lost that spot to Monica Seles, and is being increasingly pressed by Gabriela Sabatini and Arantaxa Sanchez Vicario.

Tennis history teaches a clear lesson. If the number-one player wants to stay number one, he or she must be flexible about his or her game. Every other top player shapes his or her game in order to beat number one, which in fact dictates to some degree how tennis is taught around the country at a particular time.

In this regard, Seles offered some acute observations after

a match in Palm Springs that I covered in February 1992. "Sure, I know they're all out there, looking for ways to knock me off," she said. "That's why I've got to keep thinking and stay ahead of them with my plans."

When she was asked what specifically she had in mind, she replied, smiling: "I'm not about to tell you that. But obviously, I've got to develop an all-court game because if they get better than me at the baseline, I've got to be able to put pressure on them from the net."

The greatest champions have been able to adjust to changing opponents, as well as changing court conditions. Jack Kramer is considered the creator of the modern serve and volley game, which is especially effective on fast courts. And most people credit him with that style of play only. Yet, when I asked him about it, Jack said he very rarely lost to Pancho Gonzales on clay, a slow surface, certainly a measure of his flexibility.

Rod Laver twice won the Grand Slam, which consists of the Australian, French, and U.S. Opens and Wimbledon. Which meant winning on grass, clay, and hard courts.

Competitiveness

You can modulate the degree of competition you allow into your game. You can work through in your own mind just what competition means to you, how much you are comfortable with, how much you want to compete with yourself and against others. But, tennis is inherently competitive.

I have encountered people who are stable and thoughtful and have decided that in the end all they want to do when they play is hit. They don't even keep score. I have tremendous respect for them because they have worked through a knotty problem and arrived at their own healthy, independent solution. But I have encountered many more people who have not thought it through and who avoid competition as a defensive mechanism.

However you resolve this, in my opinion you will enjoy tennis considerably more if you have a reasonable tolerance for competition. Otherwise, the game can be too disturbing.

After all, if an opponent is playing to win and hitting balls intended to penetrate your weaknesses, and all you want to do is stand at the baseline and hit pretty forehands, you soon will be forced into a form of passive frustration, irritation, anger. For most of us, that's no fun. You can, of course, play only with people who also do not want to compete. (More on this interesting, important aspect of mental tennis in Chapter 8.)

CHAPTER 6

How to Get What You Want from Tennis

IN THE LAST CHAPTER, I suggested you do something simple, yet few players do it: think about why you play tennis and what you expect from the game.

If you do, you'll create a mental map and plan that will provide you with a fresh perspective on yourself and your game. Then you'll approach tennis with much greater clarity and direction. Then you'll be able to say, "Here's what I'm after, here's what I have to work on to get there."

Even if it turns out on reflection that your goals are quite modest, the understanding and insight you'll gain from such an exercise will leave you feeling better about playing.

Take it a step further. Once you've answered those basic questions and clarified your goals — hopefully, realistic goals — think about two keys to getting from tennis what you want: the right attitude and the right coach.

The Right Attitude: Be Selfish

I've referred to this idea a few times in the book. Let me spell out my thoughts.

If you really want to enjoy tennis and succeed at it, however you define "succeed," develop what I call healthy selfishness. It means, among other things, that you play for yourself.

It means that how you look to other people while you are playing does not matter much.

Sure, where self-esteem is involved, we all like compliments. But when you are healthily selfish, even if you appear slow and awkward to others, that means less and less to you because you are wrapped up in your own objectives. And they are so much more important to you than the fleeting opinions of others. On one level, you don't even care if other people beat you. You are playing with your own goals and pleasures in mind.

For example, let's say you are trying to get the swing on your forehand right. That's all that matters to you today. You want the Ivan Lendl Loop. That's what you're concentrating on. Being able to work on that, to feel that you are hitting it better, perhaps even to put some shots away, will bring considerable pleasure to you.

When you play that way and receive real satisfaction, regardless of the score, then you are being selfish in a positive and healthy way.

You are playing tennis for your own healthy reasons. And that is one of the secrets to pleasure in tennis or any sport. Everyone I have seen play this way has made dramatic gains.

In the previous chapter, I mentioned the surprising results of the survey on the reasons people offered for playing tennis.

In fact, people who try to learn the game because they think it will bring them the approval and love of a mate — people who are incapable of being healthily selfish and pursuing their own needs and desires — those people are increasing their chances for tennis failure and psychological failure.

The stress of trying to learn under those conditions will keep them from being able to experiment and learn, keep them from being able to go through the slow, difficult, awkward process of making mistakes and learning a new sport, which is never easy in adult life.

Usually their motivation will not be strong enough to keep them going. There simply won't be enough gratification for them in those frustrating early stages. They won't be playing well enough to gain inner satisfaction from their strokes and their progress. And they won't have reached a level at which they feel they bring credit to their spouse. Or one at which their spouse begins to give them the kinds of honest compliments for which they profoundly yearn.

Though this is changing somewhat, it still seems to me that among the people who come to the tennis college, more women than men approach the sport with this shaky motivation, which is hardly surprising in our culture. "I want to play tennis with my husband," a woman will say, "and frankly I'm embarrassed to be on the court with him."

I try to explain to these women that even though I can certainly understand their wanting to play with their husbands, unfortunately I don't think that's going to be sufficient motivation, or provide them with sufficient pleasure. I try to explain that to make this work they must play for themselves, for their own good reasons. They must want to learn to improve themselves, to develop skills, their own skills.

In other words, I tell each woman to be selfish about herself and to satisfy her own needs. You are a person, I remind them. You can enjoy the learning process itself and enjoy the pleasure that you will feel as you improve. If you approach it that way, you will become a better player, and eventually, if you choose, you can play on the same court with your husband with no fear of embarrassment.

Looked at another way, if you try to play tennis for someone else, then you're going to set yourself up for a number of problems and failures.

Every time you make a mistake, it will seem as if you are

letting that other person down. Imagine how debilitating that might be.

In the end, you cannot play tennis for your husband, for your mother or your father. You cannot play even for your team. You first must play for yourself, and then your team and others will benefit.

If you are playing first for your team, what happens if you start to lose? You feel that you are letting your team down. And that burden grows heavier.

However, if you play for yourself with a healthy attitude, you'll play as well as you can play. If you win, fine. That adds to your pleasurable feelings and it also helps your team's score. If you lose, you still helped your team because you gave it your best. And if you did that, it usually means you enjoyed a good tough match and pushed yourself further than you did the day before. Probably, you felt some improvement on that forehand. Probably, tomorrow you will go out and do it again and not only win in personal terms, but in match terms as well. So you will win doubly — for yourself and for your team.

Hu Na, the Chinese tennis star who defected to the United States, provides a fairly dramatic example of what I mean about the importance of being selfish.

In 1979, I went to China and helped train coaches and players in a joint project of the Professional Tennis Association and the United Nations. While there, I worked with Hu Na, then the junior champion of China. Two years later, she became China's number-one woman player. Number one in a country of almost one billion people is pretty good.

Not long after, Hu Na defected and came to see me. She was confused and generally in terrible emotional shape. Here she was, the best woman player in China, yet she couldn't win a single qualifying match to get herself into a tournament in the United States. At the same time, as a defector, she had become the center of an international incident. She had six camera crews chasing her everywhere. Not surprisingly, she could not concentrate on her tennis.

To make matters worse, she had a game that depended greatly on the way she rolled her racket head. If you play that way and your mind and body are not functioning right, your game is going to be just slightly off. You will lose one match after another because that kind of racket-control game requires total accuracy. And pressures of the sort Hu Na was suffering are exactly what throws such a game off.

When she came to see me in California, I sat down with her and told her that I thought there was something more important than working on her strokes at the moment, and that was working on her state of mind. I told her that I admired her and I respected very much what she had done. It was a courageous act, I said, and she seemed to me a first-rate human being. Further, I let her know that I cared about her as a human being. Whether she ever won a tennis match again in her life had nothing to do with my feelings for her.

I said that to her because I meant it and also because I wanted to remove a pressure I was sure she felt — that I would only like her and help her if she became a big success as a tennis player.

Champions get that all the time. They are dismissed as human beings and to some degree, they dismiss themselves. "I am only as good as my last win, my last championship. People only like me because I'm a champion. Nobody likes me because I'm a good person. Nobody likes me because I'm bright, because I'm funny, because I'm nice to other people. They only like me because I'm a star."

I wanted Hu Na to understand that I did not want anything from her. I did not want her money. I did not want fame from becoming her coach.

As we talked, I turned the conversation to the matter of selfishness. I sensed that we had to address it, if she was going to make real progress with herself on the professional circuit and in her new culture.

I asked her what she felt when she went out to play for China.

"First, you play for the glory of China and the Communist Party," she replied, though she was not a member of the Communist Party. "Then, for the team. Then, you play for yourself."

"Okay," I said, "let's try to reverse that. Let's turn that upside down so that you begin to play for yourself. China and the party and the team, they will all receive their fair share of glory. But first you play for yourself. Because I think having a billion people on your back is kind of a heavy load."

It didn't happen overnight. Hu Na worked with me for a little over two months, and she began to understand what I was after. We talked and talked. And we also worked hard on her game. She had to change three or four strokes completely, which is very tough to accomplish. But she worked hard, and unquestionably she was a talented player. She was also blessed with a perfect body for tennis, an Arthur Ashe body: tall, lean, fast.

I'm very proud that in that year she progressed from the point of not being able to win a qualifying match, to reaching the second round at the U.S. Open and the third round at Wimbledon.

It was a great, great achievement for her. She was, however, only able to lift her game over what it had been in China when she began to realize that she, herself, was a person. And that she could concentrate on herself, on her own game, on her own strokes, and when she was playing put aside the responsibility and burden of representing one billion people.

Or one husband.

The Right Coach

Children can go quite far with baseball, football, and basketball without any coaching. These are also sports that are widely available, played in backyards, streets, playgrounds, and gyms all over America.

Tennis courts are limited, however, and more important, tennis is not a sport many people can teach themselves.

If you recall what we considered in Chapter 2 on the development of software packages in the brain, it is clear that good instruction at the earliest stages of learning the game yields results and eliminates the need for extensive relearning processes later.

But successful learning only works if the coach is right, and right in two ways:

- He or she must have the data you need to learn and improve.
- He or she must suit you psychologically.

Let's discuss six criteria and qualities you should look for and expect in a coach.

1. Is the coach knowledgeable?

What a tennis coach knows has nothing to do with the tournaments he has won, which is what you will probably hear about when you ask an inexperienced coach about his background.

Of course, most people don't even ask. Perhaps they don't think they have that right. But they do, and it's important to ask in order to get a sense of where the coach is coming from, as well as where he hopes to lead you. Where did he learn to teach? Does he have a particular approach to teaching? An educational style, a philosophy? What kinds of goals does he have for his students?

When students ask me that kind of question, I explain that above all I want to help students reach their highest levels of performance as well as enjoyment, and do so in the shortest period of time. And I tell them — warn them — that this usually means changing strokes and perspectives, too.

Underlying everything is a special goal: to help them maintain or heighten their self-esteem.

If you hear that kind of response from me or any instructor, you get a sense of approach. You might not like it. You might prefer someone who says: "There are seven basic strokes. I start with the serve . . ."

Know what you are looking for. If you don't feel comfortable with your coach's response to your questions about himself and his approach, get yourself another instructor.

It's amazing to me the number of accomplished, bright people who assume a tennis instructor knows everything. Perhaps it's because we all grow up with such strong authority figures for coaches in sports.

I have taught countless physicists, for example, who confessed they had never questioned a pro who had told them that the higher they threw the toss, the more time they would have to hit the serve.

That, however, is contrary to the law of gravity, and these are people who can tell you about the gravity parabola on Mars, not to mention that on Earth. They put vehicles in space. Yet, until I told them to lower the toss to the peak, the apex of their reach in order to give themselves more time, they never thought that, of course, the higher they threw the ball, the faster it would fall, so the less time the ball would be in the striking zone for them to hit it. They had never questioned the pro who defied the law of gravity.

2. Does the pro have a rationale for nearly everything he/she is teaching?

If a coach asks you to do a drill and you don't understand the connection between that drill and your game of tennis, you have every right to ask her, why? What's the usefulness of this drill?

The coach should not be threatened by such a question (nor should that be your intent). Neither should she assume an attitude and provide an answer that is essentially not an answer but an assertion of authority. If she says, "Because that's the way I teach," thank her and walk off the court. You are removing yourself from a learning climate that will turn hostile and unproductive, that will only produce frustration and anger in you.

If she says, however, "I want you to get into the habit of keeping the racket head vertical at the impact point for this shot," and provides a slow demonstration, or, "Here's why I want it tilted at this angle on this shot, even if it feels awkward at first," you should begin to develop confidence in her knowledge of her profession.

There will be times certainly when she is working on instinct. But then she should be honest with you. "You know, I can't fully explain this one to you, but I have seen it work for an awful lot of my students . . ."

But most of the time, she should have a rationale for what she is doing and asking you to do. Then you can process her explanation and integrate that data. Otherwise, you are learning by rote, and for most of us, that is a most inefficient way to learn.

We learn better in tennis, as in the rest of life, when we are given good reasons why things happen.

In my opinion, we don't question professionals in other areas of our lives enough either. However, if you went to your dentist and he started cleaning your teeth with a large piece of sandpaper, I bet you would ask him what in the world he was doing.

If your tennis coach can't give you a rationale, then you have bought witchcraft. You might turn out to be lucky. But I think you're taking a tremendous gamble. She might give you information that causes you to develop a faulty software package. It could take you months or years to erase that.

A coach, after all, who does not really know why she is teaching you a particular skill might very well not know what signature is best for you. If that happens, you will not only spend a considerable amount of money to develop the wrong package, you will have to spend another bundle to correct it.

On the other hand, I don't think you can pay a good coach enough. After all, she gives you something that provides you with pleasure for the rest of your life. But a bad coach ought to pay you for messing you up.

3. Is the coach's personal teaching style right for you?

We respond differently to different instructors.

Though I have no use for it, I've had people tell me they like their coach to yell at them like a Marine sergeant. I think most people find such treatment abusive. They want a supportive coach.

Whatever suits you, do not simply accept an instructor's style.

Before you start working with an instructor, tell him which style you prefer. That not only provides him with an important piece to the whole learning process, it should eliminate subsequent confrontations, which are understandably tough for both students and instructors. People often tell me they find it difficult to confront an instructor once they have begun a lesson and tell him: "You know, I'll learn better, if you holler at me less."

But never forget: A good instructor will be able to adapt to the particular needs of his clients.

4. Can the coach teach you in the way that's best suited to your particular learning style?

This is terribly important and frequently overlooked, probably because most people don't have much of an idea of how they best learn.

A considerable amount of research has been done to explain how people learn. We still don't know all the answers.

What we do know is that we tend to have preferences for

one learning style over another. Some people, for example, learn faster with a predominance of visual cues. For others, having a skill explained by a visual demonstration doesn't help much. They might learn better if the coach took their arm and guided it through a stroke, allowing them to *feel* the movement.

As I said, most of us go through life learning or not learning, but never giving any thought to our own personal learning process and style.

Or about the way our brains work. Reflect on it, because that understanding is important to improving your mental tennis game.

It will enable you to approach an instructor as you never have before, and to create an extremely productive learning relationship with her. Many people are able to help themselves in this process by recalling a teacher from high school or college who taught in a manner that was especially suitable and successful for them. Then they isolate the specific teaching techniques that instructor employed, and share them with the new tennis coach.

Let me go a bit into the ways people prefer to learn. You should find yourself in one of these groups, a recognition that will help you guide your tennis-learning process.

By seeing: Some people have a preference for visual cues.

You find this frequently with children. A boy goes to a baseball game. At the end of the game he can spit just like his favorite pitcher. He's got his hat exactly the number of degrees to the right that the pitcher has his visor pointed. He can imitate the walk of that favorite pitcher. He's got all the pitcher's moves. He shifts his hips just the way the pitcher does. And when he himself goes to pitch, he will use those visual cues to simulate that pitcher's movement.

There are lots of other eight-year-old boys who might go to the same game. Indeed, sit next to our first eight-year-old, cheer madly for the same pitcher, declare that pitcher is their favorite player of all time. But if you ask that second eight-year-old to imitate the way the pitcher moves around the mound, that boy wouldn't have a clue how to do it. He simply does not possess the same visual cue system.

By doing: There are other people who learn by doing.

These are people who usually say to themselves and some-times to me: "I don't want to sit around. I don't like to listen too much. Let's just get out on the court and do it."

One problem with doers is that they work primarily on a trial-and-error basis. And trial and error is generally the slowest way to learn, unless you happen to get lucky. If the first trial you execute happens to be the right one, it works. But the right one could be the last of several, not an efficient or effective system for learning.

People who learn by trial and error often attempt things that we already know do not work. There's no point in rein-venting the wheel, especially if we know that that particular wheel is not going to work for these particular purposes.

Still, doers are doers. In both the Tennis College and the Ski College, I discovered that we had to keep the blinds drawn during classroom sessions because of doers. They sit down and in two minutes they want to get going. They can-not stand lectures or films. When they look out the window and see people headed for the tennis courts or the chair lift, they go berserk. "Hey, there's another guy starting to play! Let's go! What are we waiting for?" And once they're in that state of mind, they don't hear anything you're trying to teach them.

Doers are extremely uncomfortable with a holistic approach to learning tennis, or any sport. Since the holistic method is my own preference, I often suggest to them that they are not going to get their money's worth in my class, that they would be much better off thinking through their tennis problems and then coming back, or going elsewhere for private lessons. Then, an instructor can work with them on those well-defined problems, and those alone. Taking the broader holistic approach completely disorients a doer.

By hearing: Presumably, we all listen while learning. But there are some predominantly auditory learners who prefer to close their eyes during a lecture and only *listen* for cues. Visual cues seem to throw them off. But not all tasks can be learned through auditory means alone.

By parts: There's another kind of learner that I call the thinker or engineer type. This is a person who has got to see all of the different elements and sequences in a process and put them in relationship to each other. Segment 1, segment 2, segment 3 — how are these connected? How will I know if I've arrived at point 2, 3, or 4?

You must give these people good data, and usually you cannot possibly give them too much. They are capable of handling and manipulating great numbers of variables at the same time. Of course, many people cannot operate this way, can handle only one element at a time.

The most successful system for teaching any sport that I've found — and surely some will challenge this — is the Gestalt process. In psychology, Gestalt is a methodology in which an integrated whole is greater than the sum of its parts. For our purposes, it means grasping individual elements and understanding how they relate; putting it all together in your mind, so you see the whole.

It's my experience that people learn tennis better when they see the whole picture, all its individual components, and understand how these components relate. Some people can be given bigger bites of information than others, but the process remains the same.

Instructing with this perspective is also nicely compatible with my general teaching philosophy: to emphasize long-term goals.

This approach, however, makes learning more difficult in the early stages. But in my experience, if students are given sufficient support in those difficult beginning stages, when they catch up they will be light-years ahead of players seeking only short-term goals.

We tested this by dividing students into two groups. In one, the students were taught essentially by rote, basically by memorizing specific steps, but were not taught the theory and substance behind what they were doing. There was obviously no attempt to give them a full picture.

They learned to get their rackets back and step into the ball as they hit it. Bring the racket back, step, and swing. Racket back, step, swing. Racket back, step, swing.

They did quite well at first, better than the beginners of the second group, who were learning by first absorbing the whole big picture with all its variables.

By the second or third day, however, people who grasped the total picture and could see how elements related were considerably ahead of people who were in the racket back–step–swing process.

I think you can begin to see why it is important to decide how you learn best and to share that with your coach. The earlier you share it, the more problems you will avoid later.

If you have a preference for visualizing, for example, the pro should try, among other teaching techniques, to *show* you everything. If she says, "Sorry, we don't teach that way here," you want to know that very early on, before you have given her any money or time.

To avoid this with a tennis camp, call ahead. Talk through your concerns before you send them a dollar or take a costly flight to the resort. If it's a summer tennis camp for children, parents should not only call the camp but also talk to parents of children who have been there.

I recall teaching in grammar school and high school where a lot of children showed a preference for visual learning. Among them were very bright kids who nevertheless did poorly because somebody stood in front of their class saying,

"Here's the problem: Three times five divided by four . . ." The visualizers were lost. "I have to see it on paper," they would say.

On the other hand, if most visual cues do not matter to you, it will not help you a great deal simply to watch your pro or to watch a professional match. You probably will not pick up much of what he or she is doing.

In that case, you are better off gathering data. For example, Agassi made X number of crosscourt shots and down-the-line shots, and of his crosscourt shots only Y went into the net, whereas of his down-the-line shots Y plus Z went into the net. Data of that sort will allow you to learn, while that same information will mean little or nothing to the visualizer.

To repeat an important point: The good coach should respect you and your learning-style preference, and be able to work with you in the way you learn best, not impose her teaching style on you.

5. Is there mutual respect between you and your coach?

Your coach should value you as an individual, should respect your questions, responses, and feelings.

On the other hand, you should value his skills, knowledge, and qualities as a teacher and a human being. Above all, you should respect him as an educator, not a human ball machine.

Otherwise, there is not going to be much trust, openness, or honesty between the two of you, and without that there is not going to be a very healthy climate for learning, or teaching.

For lessons to be effective, you want the kind of relationship with a coach in which you are comfortable saying whatever you feel at the moment, especially if something doesn't feel right to you. Or if you don't understand a point. Or if you're not connecting with the instructor's style of teaching.

Your coach, meanwhile, must be able to accept any criticism you might have — direct or implied — of his teaching technique.

Intent is terribly important in these honest, critical exchanges. Honesty can be a weapon. If your intention is to attack and hurt the coach for whatever reason, or vice versa, then honest comments will not be related to improving your tennis but to satisfying some conscious or unconscious need. The result will probably be pain and destruction and the crumbling of the learning relationship.

I have seen instructors ridicule students, young and old, and then say, "I'm telling you this for your own good." But that humiliated student derives no good from those words, only embarrassment and anger. That instructor is using his knowledge of a student's tennis problems to satisfy his own psychological needs. If you find yourself the object of such abuse, don't put up with it for a minute.

If, however, you and the coach respect each other, then these honest exchanges will be impersonal and the result will be clarification, growth, improvement, a richer learning environment.

I've trained a vast number of instructors. I make a point of telling them how critical this kind of open exchange with their students is, that it can exist if the coach feels confident enough and comfortable enough with himself to accept criticism, to accept the feelings students are expressing and handle the affects of those feelings on themselves.

We experimented in one class, showing a video, then having the instructors ask students for feelings, questions, responses. We stressed to the instructors that we wanted immediate feedback from the students, uncensored responses. And that's what the students gave. But many of the instructors couldn't handle it. They couldn't handle the emotions it provoked in them.

As the students began talking about what they thought and felt in response to the video, instructors, without realizing it, cut them off. "Okay, fine, that's good," they'd say. "Now let's go on to the next thing."

They were not capable of dealing with their own feelings that were surfaced by the students, and so they could not openly respond to those students.

I taped the exchange and later, when I showed the instructors the tape and they saw how they had reacted, they were stunned.

In psychoanalysis this is called countertransference, what the analyst must confront in response to the thoughts and emotions that are provoked in him by a patient's statements, feelings, actions. Every good psychoanalyst knows that he must be able to understand and cope with those emotions, often quite disturbing feelings, or they will distort the analysis, perhaps even prevent his working successfully with the patient. It's one big reason good, well-trained analysts go through years of psychoanalysis themselves as part of their training, to be able to understand and cope with what the patient stirs up in them.

A good instructor, without the benefit of a training analysis, must nevertheless be able to handle countertransference. He must be able to hear you, and respond in a way that advances the learning process, even if what you say is critical of him and disturbing to him.

Similarly, there must be room in the relationship for him to be honest with you, even if that honesty might be difficult for you to accept.

It is often difficult for the coach as well, so much so that many coaches would rather avoid it and keep the relationship superficially happy. But without the truth, how can any student learn and improve? If a student is not very good and is repeating the same mistakes over and over, unless the coach is honest with the student, he will continue to make the same mistakes, deluding himself that he's playing good tennis.

I see a certain amount of this at our Tennis College, with some of the celebrities who come there. Being only ninety minutes from Los Angeles, we get a fair number of rather famous people who are in movies and television.

I remember one actor who obviously had played a lot of tennis and taken a lot of lessons. But the truth was that when he hit the ball, he was lucky to keep it in California. Of course, nobody had ever told him that. To the contrary, as I learned, all his friends and hangers-on kept telling him, "You're great! Boy, can you play!"

Well, he came to the college and he was terrible. After a while, he walked over to me and said, "I've never been in group lessons before. I think I'm distracted by the other people."

We got him a private instructor. He went out with the instructor and he still could not hit the ball. "My real problem is," he then explained, "I don't like being singled out."

The truth was that he couldn't beat Mickey Mouse. I took him into my office to talk. I wanted to be both supportive and honest with him.

"I like you and I hope what I have to say doesn't hurt you," I told him, "but it's important that I be honest with you. You're paying for the truth and my honest professional opinion and I'd like to give that to you. I think it can be helpful.

"You know," I went on, "I overheard some of your friends telling you that you were great. But after watching you, I see that you have a style of play that is tricky. It's going to allow you to hit one great shot, but probably lead to lots of terrible shots as well."

That was all true and, quite important, by the way I put it to him I was able to remove the criticism from the personal realm. We were talking about his style of play, not his personality or character.

"You're trying to hit a big topspin forehand," I explained, "and that kind of shot requires approximately a fifteen-millisecond response from you. Which is nearly impossible. As a result, you may have a good win, but you'll also have a lot of bad losses. Our goal here is to have you play well every day. You can, in fact, have a very good game, but right now, I think you're playing about two levels below what you're capable of playing."

At first, he was hurt. I could see it in his face. Nobody had ever talked to him that way.

"Look," I said, "we still love you. We're not abandoning you. To the contrary, I'm giving you the truth about your tennis game and if you stick with us, you're going to play this game and play it very well.

"If you disagree with me, if you think I'm full of it, tell me. Say anything you want to me. Ask me any questions you want."

We talked a bit, not very much. I explained further to him — and it was also the first time anybody ever had — why his particular big, sweeping, rolling forehand was such a difficult shot to execute with any consistency. And, I assured him, we could show him other ways to hit a forehand.

He began to understand, but he was shaken, no question about it, shaken right down to the bottom of his ego. But he picked himself up.

I worked with him and then one of our best instructors took over. And sure enough, the man started to hit the ball in a different, more effective way.

He ended up with a new, much better tennis game, enjoying the sport more than he ever had before, and he became one of the best unpaid publicists my Tennis College ever had.

None of it would have happened if I hadn't cared enough about him to tell him the truth. I'm afraid too many coaches would not, or they might have been intimidated by him and his reputation. They would have let him get out on the court and go through a program, then told him he was wonderful. I couldn't do that.

I noted earlier in this chapter that the truth could be a

weapon in your hands, certainly in the hands of an instructor. But in the hands of a good and mentally healthy instructor, the truth can be illuminating and yet it can be couched in supportive, specific terms.

"You're making an effort, a good effort. But you still don't have that volley yet. Your racket reached only to your hips that time, and your goal is to get the racket, ball, and your eyes all on the same level. So you're still not getting your body down quite low enough to hit that low volley. It's a tough shot, I know, I know. . . ."

Or, "You're really trying hard, I can see that, giving it your best effort, but there is something happening here where you're not reaching your potential, you're not doing as well as I think you can. . . . Maybe we need to discuss this so we both understand what this potential is, and both agree on it. Then I think you'll get to it. . . ."

6. How involved is your coach in your learning?

If you are making an honest effort to improve your game and that includes regular lessons with your coach, then it is not too much to expect her to be thinking of you and your game even after the lesson is over.

She is not your shrink nor your parent, but a good pro will be concerned about your total growth and not care only about your tennis for the hour that you're taking the lesson.

She should be coming to you and saying, "I saw so-and-so playing the other day, and I think she'd be a good match for you." Or, "It occurred to me the other night that you might benefit from playing in the Thursday night league."

She should also expect that you will practice what she is trying to teach you in those lessons, that you will try to develop new software. If she doesn't expect that, or care about it, she's showing a kind of indifference that will help you stay mired on your present plateau.

Unfortunately, a form of unhealthy codependency can easily develop between the two of you in which you are not really trying, but maintain the attitude, "So what . . . I'm paying for this lesson, we'll do it my way." And the pro falls into the trap of not caring because she sees that you don't really care, and indeed, you are still paying the fee.

A good pro confronted with a pattern like that will not roll along with it, but rather point it out to you. Just as a psychoanalyst might intervene and tell a patient that his behavior in sessions over the last couple of weeks seems to be a form of resistance to the treatment and it should be looked at, so a good tennis pro will tell her client that they are not making progress, for reasons X, Y, and Z, and that perhaps they had better consider a new plan to break this pattern.

While the good coach will expect you to respond to her effort and make an honest attempt to improve, she will not produce the results you want tomorrow. She is in the process with you for the long term. And during that time and struggle, she will help you feel comfortable feeling uncomfortable.

A productive relationship with a coach you like and trust will be a source of experimentation, of learning, of confidence.

You will probably reach out more, be more adventurous in your choice of tennis matches, which is one route to growth.

Let me suggest an experiment.

Think about the level you are aiming for. If you are now playing at a B level and you would like to move up to low-A, it will help if you know what low-A tennis consists of specifically. How much faster are the serves? How much faster are the ground strokes? How much more aggressively do you have to play?

The way to get those answers is to play against low-A players. Find some tournaments that are over your head and play in them. You might lose, but you will learn specifically what you need to do in order to raise your game.

If you can take a friend along who charts your match and

analyzes it with you, even better. Perhaps this reveals that your big problem is handling power. Maybe it's service return. Whatever it is, you can then return to your coach and start working on those particular parts of your game.

It can also be useful to play against people a level below yourself at times. Then you can learn how to close out a match, how to win.

Another way of working well with your coach is to bring to your lesson a player with a style that gives you trouble, and play a match. The pro gives the other player a few tips, in return for her effort. But the real purpose is for the pro to have a special chance to analyze your game against someone you find particularly difficult to win against.

It can be tremendously helpful. "She gives you lots of shots in mid-court and that's where your forehand is weak. That's where you're losing points. . . ."

From such an exercise, your pro can produce a list of problems and shots that you will want to work on together.

What I also like about both these ideas — playing in tournaments above your level, and bringing a difficult opponent to an exhibition lesson — is that they allow you to shape your own learning process.

You are injecting elements into the lessons that will allow you and your coach to concentrate on specific problems in your game. And they may well be problems that your coach, as good as she is, might not have picked up on. So, your efforts to expand your learning should be a help to both of you.

It also should leave you feeling good about yourself. You are the one who is making the effort. You are taking control of an aspect of your life that can produce for you a great deal of pleasure. And perhaps it is an aspect that has been producing more frustration than anything else, up to now.

But now you are actively changing that.

CHAPTER 7

How Parents, Children, and Coaches Can Get What They Want from Tennis

NOT LONG AGO, a man in a blue velour warm-up suit approached me at the Tennis College in Coto de Caza.

"Vic," he said, "I want you to teach my son so he can win a tennis scholarship to Stanford."

"Does your boy like tennis?" I asked, always my first response to such encounters.

"I think so," he replied. "I have a feeling he's a very good athlete. And I think Stanford is a terrific school."

"You go to Stanford?"

"No, but it would be a good place for Ted."

We talked for only a couple of minutes but it was clear that he and his wife had planned this with some seriousness. So, even though I don't take on children and train them to win tennis scholarships to Stanford or anywhere else, I was curious. My instincts told me that a modest intervention at this point might save another child from being warped by parents projecting their own fantasies.

"Where's your youngster?" I asked. "I'd like to meet him." Sometimes a problem like this can be helped simply by asking the child how he feels about the professed goals, in this case tennis and Stanford. The boy might really dream of swimming for the University of Vermont.

"He's right here," the man answered, and held up the

hand of the little boy standing next to him, a child of perhaps five or six. I had assumed that the boy he was talking about was at least thirteen or fourteen, at a point in life where he and the family were beginning to think seriously about college. But here was this child, probably still in kindergarten.

Perhaps this man was a bit extreme, even for a totally driven father, but in substance he was quite familiar to me.

He was a tennis parent, or an incipient tennis parent, a type that shares certain characteristics with the more famous stage parent.

Anna Freud, daughter of Sigmund, and a distinguished child psychoanalyst herself, cast some light on such people. In her book *Normality and Pathology in Childhood,* she observed that "there are parents whose attachment to the child depends on the latter's representing for them either an ideal of themselves or a figure of their own past. To retain parental love under these conditions, the child allows his personality to be molded into a pattern which is not his own and which conflicts with or neglects his own innate potentialities.

"Some mothers, or fathers, assign to the child a role in their own pathology and relate to the child on this basis, not on the basis of the child's real needs.

"Many mothers actually pass on their symptoms to their young children and subsequently act them out together with them in the form of a folie à deux. . . ."

Skeptics might accuse me of making too much of ambitious parents. But it is not possible to have coached as many children as I have and seen as many parents relate to their children over the issue of tennis not to recognize how meaningful and widespread this problem is.

It appears in many forms and on many levels of seriousness.

Certainly, when a grown man asks me to create a tennis scholarship to Stanford for his kindergarten child, that is approaching outer limits.

Yet, I frequently see parents living and dying with every

point their child plays in a tournament. One mother recently told me that she got so angry with the way her twelve-year-old was playing in a match, she simply got in her car and left. She left the tournament and her child, and headed for home, sixty miles away, with no thought of where her child would go, how she would get home, and no thought about whether the twelve-year-old might worry about her mother, imagine that she was killed in an automobile accident. This woman was so disturbed by her daughter's playing badly and losing, she abandoned her.

There are famous tennis parents who manipulate and exploit their children so egregiously and publicly, they get written about. Clearly, their children are not so much children to them as corporations, business opportunities to pull in millions of dollars. Most of these parents, of course, swear on Bibles that they are doing everything only in the best interests of their children.

Other tennis parents manage and manipulate their children with the idea of winning tennis scholarships and launching them into the professional tour. Even tournaments for children under twelve are crawling with agents as well as parents ready to bribe officials to get higher rankings for their children. Higher rankings, after all, help them win scholarships.

I regularly receive calls from parents asking me, "Who's the best agent? Who should I be looking at? My kid's got a lot of talent and I can see it coming and I just want to be out front." But it turns out their kid is eight years old. They're not really out front, they're simply getting an early start at counting dollars.

It's quite grotesque. I saw an unintended parody of the whole sad, corrupt business recently in a tournament in California at which the father of one young player, being touted by the national press, was trying to charge a fee of anyone who wanted to take a photo of his child. A fairly primitive form of commercialization, probably a violation of the child labor laws, but the fellow had the right idea: the bottom line is, make money off one's child.

Talking with any number of tennis parents, it seems apparent to me that they have no idea of the damage they are inflicting on their children. Yet, any child who is the object of that kind of treatment by his or her parents is probably going to suffer and pay a terrible psychic price.

The parents are quite unaware of their own ambitions, of how much of themselves they have invested in having their children succeed.

Not surprisingly, there is little honest communication between these parents and their children. Often the children accept the role assigned them by their parents for fear of losing their love if they don't, or the parents are deaf to any statements from their children about their true feelings. I've lost track of the number of times I've asked a child, "Do you like tennis?," only to have a parent answer, "Oh, God, does she love tennis." That tells me something about the parent, but nothing about the child.

For a video on the subject, I interviewed and taped a number of children and their tennis mothers, usually the parent who drives the child to tournaments. The disparate exchanges of one mother and her daughter were typical. The daughter was ranked, yet at the time was thinking about dropping out of tennis.

"What do you want from your daughter?" I asked the mother.

"Well, I just want her to enjoy the sport for sport's sake," she answered. "To have some fun. To relax. To just have nice experiences."

Then, away from the mother, I interviewed the daughter. "What do you want?"

"All I want is my mom to just let me enjoy this sport."

At another point in her interview, the mother was talking

about her daughter's upsetting body language. "When my daughter loses a point, she walks back with her head down."

In her interview, the girl commented: "I'm afraid to look up because every time I've lost a point my mother's up there, going, like, 'Oh, no, not again.' You know?"

Both mother and daughter were stunned when we showed them the tapes of their interviews. They both felt they were a mother and daughter who cared about the other. Neither could believe that she had misread the other so fully.

Reevaluate Winning

Surely, one of the most important messages parents convey to their children is the meaning of winning. All too frequently, it is an overemphasis on winning and often it is a message sent quite unconsciously.

How often you hear a parent say to his or her child: "I just want you to do the best you can and be the best person you can be."

But when that same child goes home, what does the child hear as soon as he or she goes through the door? "You win? How'd you do today? Did you win? Or lose?"

The kid gets the true message the parent is conveying: Winning is everything. Those are the values wrapped in that win-or-lose question, applied to every aspect of the child's life — grades, sports, date for the prom, and, heaven help us, college.

Further, the child lives in a society that perpetuates and glorifies the attitude that winning is everything. In sports, the child encounters it in its most naked form.

When children win, quite understandably, parents brag. But how rare it is to hear a parent brag about the effort a child made, regardless of the result. Indeed, normally if the child loses, the parent changes the conversation.

Think what the difference might be if instead of asking the child, "Did you win today?," the parent asks, "Did you learn anything today?" With that shift of emphasis, the parent creates a different world.

First of all, you convey to the child that you care about more than winning in the traditional sense. You are saying to your child that what matters most is learning. Trying to execute the right way. Improving. Growing. Enjoying.

Countless people, however, are so hooked on results that they never have discovered the pleasure in the learning process itself. To experiment and to learn are beautiful goals. They lead to better tennis, and also eliminate any overemphasis on winning.

If you ask the question "Did you learn?" rather than "Did you win?" you will also be conveying to the child the healthy idea that he is not going to win all his matches and he is not going to lose all his matches.

Obviously, these ideas reach beyond tennis. The need to win affects us on all levels of our lives.

A friend told me recently that she and her husband had moved their son and daughter from one private school to another. The first school had a reputation for being fairly traditional and quite demanding and for placing its graduates in highly regarded colleges, all of which appealed to my friends. In fact, it appealed to them more than they realized. They were both quite successful overachievers, and they simply assumed that their children would be the same.

Their children were bright, but they had difficulties with the school, a totally nonsupportive place. The attitude of the school seemed to be: We have a terrific curriculum; if you can handle it, you'll go to Harvard; if you can't, that's your problem.

No matter how hard my friend's children worked, they seemed to slip further behind. They began to feel worse and worse about themselves, fell increasingly silent about school, and distanced themselves from their parents.

Not a moment too soon, my friends realized what was happening. They found another school that also had a good curriculum, and also made demands on its students, but reasonable demands in which teachers were extremely supportive of each student, where the heart of its educational process was not the curriculum but the individual student. This school also placed its students in respectable colleges, but very very few were even interested in applying to Harvard. That was not their definition of success, of winning.

My friend told me that part of going through the whole process with their children forced her and her husband to reexamine their own attitudes. What really mattered to them insofar as their children were concerned? An Ivy League school at all costs? Or the self-esteem of their children?

She and her husband realized that they had quite unconsciously chosen "Ivy League school" and its symbol of superiority, of success and winning, and sent that message to their children. Like so many tennis parents I have seen, they had decided that their children would win, even if the process shattered them. With that insight, the realization of how their own egos and pride were projected onto their children, they were able, finally, to understand their mistake and make the change of schools.

The results for children and parents were, according to my friend, profound. The children flourished. The family, which had been battered by the problems the children were bringing home, repaired itself. The parents, who had suffered an awful strain on their marriage, recovered stronger than ever. They also came up with a new motto: "Just say no to Harvard."

I learned an important lesson in the early years of my coaching career. I learned from looking at the faces of children who had lost, when I asked them that terrible question, "Did you win?"

As I thought about it, I realized what I was doing, where I was placing all of the emphasis. On winning.

That forced me to reevaluate myself as a coach and to think more deeply about my goals. I came to understand, among other things, that if a student of mine lost a match, the truth of the matter was that I was upset because I had a lot of myself wrapped up in those wins and losses. I had been saying to myself: "That dude's representing *me* out there."

Once I had flushed those thoughts from the recesses of my mind, out where I could examine them, I knew that my own values as a coach were really twisted. I had to ask myself: "Where are we — myself, the coach, and you, the student — and where are we trying to go?"

I was a coach, but I was also a teacher. I knew that I was trying to do more than instruct children how to strike a tennis ball. I was trying to help them enrich and enhance their lives. So, if a student has learned something while playing a match, he is indeed enriching and enhancing his life. And if he has achieved that in the course of the match, then he has won. Indeed, he has won something much more important than just a game of tennis. The score doesn't matter. He has won even if the score indicates that he lost the match.

Once I realized that, I began to approach students differently and something terribly important and fascinating occurred. I was able to get my students to start thinking that way too, and when they did, they began to win more matches. And now I mean "win" in terms of scores.

That was unexpected, certainly, but on reflection, quite logical. I was removing from their minds the pressures and anxieties of, above all else, having to win a match. Once they were free of that burden, they could concentrate on their tennis. They could concentrate on taking care of their problems with strokes and strategies on the court. They could identify the real problems in their games, concentrate on those problems, and come up with solutions to them.

Parents and Coaches

If a parent is deeply neurotic, there isn't much the tennis coach can do. The coach is not a therapist, neither for the parent nor the child, but the coach can guard against becoming a helping party to the neurotic process.

Obviously, there are countless parents who are not blindly destructive, who have reasonable ambitions for their children when they put their children into tennis programs. For them, if the coach is intelligent and sensitive, the two can collaborate fruitfully to create a very healthy experience for the child.

From my years of teaching children, I have found that to do this, usually the coach must first overcome his own urge to keep parents out of his tennis program.

Generally, coaches in all sports like to control. They enjoy the feeling of power they receive from shaping people, from having students respond to their commands.

They have a huge amount of power. They assume critical roles in the minds and lives of their students and can emotionally maim a young person. I've lost track of the number of tales I've heard from adults about coaches who so threatened and humiliated these people when they were growing up that they never fully overcame their scars and injuries.

I've heard parents say, "It's just so awful. I just think the coach doesn't like my kid. And every night it's so miserable. It's a nightmare around our place. We sit at the table and our kid has tears in his eyes because he's not getting into games and the coach treats him so badly."

Any parent who senses that his child is being subjected to a punishing coach should act quickly to determine what is really going on. If in fact the coach is damaging the child, the parent has, in my view, a double responsibility: first, to remove the child from the destructive environment; second, to report and/or try to remove the coach. To me, such coaches are actually engaged in a form of child abuse, and it is commonly found with coaches who are driven to win at all cost.

But a coach's power and influence over a child certainly

does not have to be harmful, by any means. Indeed, if the coach and parents can work together, that power and influence can be extremely beneficial to the child. But to reach that relationship, both coach and parents have to want it.

Frequently, I find, the qualities that attract a coach to power lead to a confrontation between him and parents. The coach wants to run his classes his way, without parents interfering.

But when a coach acts in that manner and bans parents from watching his classes, quite naturally they resent it. "I'm paying $45 an hour," they say, "and I can't even see what's going on? That's ridiculous."

Not long after I started teaching, I became aware of that coach's attitude in myself. So I reexamined how I was teaching and how I was relating to parents, and I changed my way of working. I began to hold introductory sessions for parents. They were not very different from a Parents' Orientation Night at any school in September.

I told them that I was an educator with a number of goals, and explained how I tried to teach. We talked about all I hoped to cover on the tennis court — the fundamentals of strokes, and strategy — and the other developmental goals I had.

Certainly, I explained, I looked at these classes as an opportunity for their children to relate to other children, and to learn something about handling frustration, to learn to stick with a new effort, like a different way of serving, even if success did not come early or easily.

I listened to the parents and their concerns, their expectations for the classes, their hopes for their children.

Coaches tend to forget that no one knows a child better than his or her parents. Parents can be a great resource for a coach, providing him with insights into a child that he can factor into his teaching techniques. And, of course, they can provide support for the whole tennis-learning process.

By enlisting the parents in the process rather than shutting them out, the coach can also place himself in a position of prevention, rather than one of treatment. The coach will give himself a chance to anticipate difficulties with the child.

With that in mind, I told the parents that I welcomed opportunities to chat with them, especially if their children were going through rough patches in other parts of their lives. At those times, it would be extremely helpful if they could let me know, for example, that a child was losing his appetite, or his grades were dropping, or a friendship has come apart.

At times like that, it can mean a great deal to a child if a tennis coach says to her, "Your mom tells me you're really worried about maybe having to move away next year . . . ," possibly having a brief conversation after class with the child. Not that the coach replaces a parent or, as I've said, a therapist, but he can comfort the student, and demonstrate that there is another adult ready to give support.

Also, of course, there may be times when a child's problems away from the court will affect his or her attitude during classes, and a forewarned coach can adjust.

A parent might call and say, "We don't know what's happening. But something's going on at school, and she is way down on herself." Knowing that the girl's self-esteem has been somehow battered, the coach can become especially supportive. It can help the girl get through a lesson, feel a little better about herself. It won't root out the deeper problem underlying the loss of self-esteem, but that is not the coach's job, or what his training enables him to do.

A cooperative relationship of this sort also assists a coach if disciplinary problems arise. Many children become quite adept at playing one authority figure against another. But if a disruptive child threatens to launch his mother into the fray, the coach can break up that process if he can confidently reply to the child, "Do I want to meet with your mother about this? I would welcome it. Would you like me to meet with her alone, or would you like to join us? Actually, I'd prefer that, the three of us sitting down together. But we can do it any way you feel most comfortable."

If parents come to lessons and classes and try to coach, or otherwise become obstacles to learning, then the coach has little choice but to explain to them what is happening.

And, I do mean "explain." Often, I have found, parents are completely unaware of how disruptive they are being. So, the coach can point out to them: "I'm afraid that by making comments during the lesson, showing your anger at your daughter while she's playing, your comments and facial expressions are really interfering with the class. . . . It's very difficult for me to teach your daughter under these circumstances, and for her to learn. . . . I understand that lessons can produce disappointments. It can be that way for your child, too. It's not easy to be disappointed with yourself, and still have to hit the next ball, and then have to relate to a parent. . . . So, come and watch and enjoy. Unless perhaps watching your daughter simply is too emotional and upsetting for you, and in that case, I'm afraid it's not in anyone's best interest for you to be here."

Frequently, a parent will confess that she never even realized she was making remarks or faces, and says she'll control herself, though often she removes herself from the sessions. If a parent, however, flatly denies such behavior, or disagrees with the coach's appraisal, then the honest coach has to be firmer.

In my experience it's best for the coach to take her aside, or schedule a special meeting, and then, without being accusatory, describe the disturbing behavior on her part that he has witnessed during classes. If she takes offense, denies, insists on her right to behave as she pleases — in other words, if for whatever reason she maintains that she sees nothing disruptive in her behavior and intends to continue — then I think the coach faces the very difficult task of explaining that he seriously disagrees. In fact, he has to explain that such behavior in his view is so disruptive of her child's whole learning process, that it would be better if she found another coach and class.

If the relationship between a coach and parents is strong, however, they will support each other and work together for the child's benefit.

That is what matters: the child's best interests. And that might very well mean not developing a tournament winner. Rather, it might mean supporting a physically awkward child enough so that for the first time he can play a sport and not feel ridiculous or humiliated. Imagine the lift to a child's self-esteem if he can finally achieve that, overcome that terrible hurdle in life.

Healthy parents don't need to satisfy their own needs by exploiting their children. Healthy parents are able to keep their children's needs clearly in focus. These are the parents who talk with coaches not about rankings, but about development and pleasure. Is she happy when she's playing? Is she making progress? How is she handling competition? Is she making friends? How does she feel about her tennis? About herself?

As I talk to coaches in the tennis world, I find an increasing number who feel the need for a course to help parents evaluate their own behavior, to be able to recognize when their behavior is neurotic and not in the child's best interests.

And in fact I am developing such a course. It will be one that discusses what, so far as tennis is concerned, is best for a six-year-old or an eight-year-old, a ten-year-old or a twelve-year-old, or an adolescent. A course that will provide parents with an honest view of what tournament play entails, of the possible effects on their children and themselves. A course that will enable them to recognize when they are out of control.

I am in the process of creating both the course and a system for implementing it in a number of nations around the world.

If it all comes together, it will be in my mind a course that could actually save the lives of an awful lot of children.

It has a chance of succeeding, too, because there are so many wonderful parents who want to grow along with their children.

CHAPTER 8

Healthy Changes

WE ALL HIT STRETCHES when our game seems to be coming apart.

I don't mean merely the disappearance of a normally dependable forehand or sudden trouble with overheads, which you normally devour.

I am speaking of profound malaise. A period when you don't seem to be doing much of anything right. A period, furthermore, when you can't seem to improve. An awful plateau.

The cure requires a mind-body approach.

You will probably find that you have to make adjustments to your strokes. Out of nowhere you will discover, for example, that you have turned a once solid forehand into a strange wrist shot.

You will also require a fresh perspective on the mental glitches that have arisen.

The No-Improvement-Plateau Blues

I have a writer friend who struggles wonderfully and happily with her spirited B-level game. Though I can't imagine her not writing, she maintains that if she got rich, she would put her computer aside and do nothing but take lessons. She would take tennis lessons every day, as well as piano lessons and Greek lessons. Maybe find a Greek tennis pro and combine the two.

Why lessons, as a dream? Because, she explains, with lessons she feels she is continually renewing herself and growing.

There's a lot of wisdom in that. Some people take tennis lessons with fairly mechanical objectives in mind. They want to improve strokes, period. Then they experience a wonderful surprise. Even though they hadn't anticipated it, they enjoy that marvelous feeling of personal achievement.

But what happens when the improvement seems to stop and growth seems to end?

These are debilitating and somewhat confusing periods. It's possible, especially at the beginning of these stretches, actually to play reasonably well — not at your usual level, perhaps, but still with a semblance of a game. Nonetheless, you know that something is wrong.

Obviously, your instructor is going to be instrumental in your recovery. But do not throw yourself moaning at his or her feet. Do not plead hopelessness and ask to be straightened out.

Being active, not passive, is going to be an important part of your recovery.

Start by dissecting your game yourself. And be as specific as you can.

If indeed one of the problems is the collapse of your once completely dependable forehand, be precise. Are you hitting high balls into the net and low balls over the baseline? Are baseline strokes okay, but you can't hit an approach shot? Being precise will help your instructor attack the problem with you.

Try to be objective. We all have a tendency to remember the big shots and forget the lousy ones. If we knock off three splendid aces in a match, we start thinking our serve is strong and wonderful. We blank out the nine double-faults we also hit in that match.

The best of players fall victim to this. I recall one match in which Agassi won points on six drop shots, but also missed fourteen of them. When I interviewed him afterward, he commented on how effective his drop shots had been that day.

At times like these, a videotape of a match can be tremendously helpful. As crude as the tape may be, once you see yourself on it, you will begin to see movements and problems you never suspected. We all have images of ourselves as we play, often idealized images that have little to do with the way we actually look. But there on the tape you will begin to make discoveries.

For example, even though you don't recall when it started, and are not aware of when you do it, you discover that you have stopped turning sideways to the net when you hit, and on nearly every shot you are now standing flat-footed, facing the net, with no body rotation.

Or you are not throwing the toss for the serve out nearly as far as you imagined; in fact, it's almost back by your ear.

Or you are not moving soon enough for the ball; you are late on nearly every shot. Your head is moving, following the ball, but your feet are not.

You can pick out problems and your pro should be able to analyze your play as well. People used to send me their tapes and I'd put a voice-over on them, analyzing their games, and send them back.

Notice that all these suggestions require action on your part. Active participation is critical to your recovery.

Breaking out of Slumps

There's a difference between the existential collapse I'm discussing and a slump.

In a slump, your whole game does not disintegrate, but you do find yourself losing to players you normally beat, and losing over and over.

Often players don't recognize the pattern.

Stefan Edberg said that he was having troubles at the end of 1990 and early 1991, but he couldn't figure out what was happening. Then he went to the 1991 U.S. Open.

In addition to his mysterious slump, he was further concerned because he had never done terribly well in New York. So, he entered the tournament worrying about his recent losing performances and providing himself with a self-fulfilling prophecy: "I never play well here."

Then he found himself in a fourth-round match against Michael Chang, with Chang as usual chasing down just about everything Edberg could hit. At a critical point in the match, Edberg said to himself: "This is where you usually let up. Don't. Get in there and fight." And that, Edberg told me, was the turning point for him. "Instead of just kind of dropping out and letting the match go downhill, I hung in and I won. And then I knew that I needed to be tougher. That was the match that turned me around and gave me a great attitude to go forward."

What he did, he subsequently realized, was to assume responsibility for his own behavior on the court, a good model for all players. The match against Chang was his to win or lose, the same as matches are for countless club players every day who are faced with the choice of sustaining an effort or collapsing.

Edberg got on to himself. That was all he needed, that one insight, that one match. No more slump.

In fact, he told me, what he learned from that experience carried him right through to the U.S. Open title that year.

Significantly, in 1992, he demonstrated that he had fully integrated that great lesson. He not only won the title once again, but this time he triumphed in three five-set matches. Each of them was a severe test of his will and determination.

In each, he had to fight back from being down a service break in the final set. His semifinal victory came over, once again, the determined Michael Chang. Edberg did not ever "let up," not for five hours and twenty-six minutes, apparently the longest match in the history of the tournament.

Sometimes you can break a slump with a change of venue. Lay off the game for a week or two. Then come back.

When you do, you'll enjoy a new level of excitement in playing, and probably find yourself tremendously relaxed, so relaxed you might astonish yourself with your level of play. Normally that level will drop off a bit after the first day, when your old habits start to reemerge, but you should at least feel fresh, that you are giving yourself a new start.

Change the Learning Environment

This next important step to recovery can be difficult. Very often recovery means changing your relationship with your coach, even changing roles to some extent.

This might start by your taking greater control of the lesson.

Let's assume that you have quite thoroughly analyzed your game and your problems. You have thought through matches and viewed tapes. You know what some, if not all, of your troubles are. It is time for you to tell the pro what you want to work on and why.

Also, if you haven't already, tell her how you feel. Your problems on the court might very well have reached beyond simple frustration. You might be depressed by your failures. Your pro cannot know what you are thinking and feeling unless you tell her. Do that, not expecting miracles, but as a way to guide her on how she can best work with you.

Your pro might supplement your plan, which can only help. But you have taken control of the lesson, just as you have taken control of the reconstruction of your game.

Most important at these times, keep the learning situation honest. You need honest critiques from your pro, not ego massages. Unfortunately, many instructors misinterpret their own roles at difficult stretches like this and think the best thing they can do for a student is to bolster sagging confidence with false praise and phony compliments. But there is no gain in that. A temporary alleviation, perhaps. But the problems will persist.

You might also find at such times that you want to change your relationships with certain tennis friends. Most people tend to play with the same circle of friends. Now is a time when you want to be sure that none of these people is pulling you down.

Often people knock your game, when unconsciously they are attacking you. "I just don't like the way you're playing," someone at the courts tells you. It's a remark that suggests concern. When you're actually playing well, such comments slide right off you. But when you're down, wrestling with the collapse of life on the court, that sort of comment is simply hostile. Let the remark and the person who made it slide right out of your life.

What you need in periods like this is support and good information. What you do not need is destructive criticism.

Many professional players have told me that they learn who their friends are when they start to lose. When they are winning, people are all over them. When they are losing, the phone stops ringing.

Perhaps it might be time for that very most difficult change, a change in instructors.

Don't rush into this. Don't change for the sake of change under the mistaken notion that any action is better than the status quo. But be honest with yourself. You might have had an increasing number of questions and reservations about your pro as your game has improved.

Or you might have found increasingly that while his technical proficiency remained adequate, you were having more and more problems with his personal style. You might well have gone through a stage during which you had such a low opinion of your game, such low self-esteem on the court, that any attention you got and any improvement you made seemed wondrous. From the beginning, this coach might not have been the right teacher for you, and you acknowledged that some of the instructor's personal qualities rubbed you the wrong way. Still, on balance, you felt the relationship was productive and worth sustaining.

That is not uncommon, when the student does' not feel strong enough to speak up. But finally, the moment comes when the need for change is too compelling for you to continue.

You must decide what is best for you.

Frequently, this is difficult because the student has put herself into a position of dependency. She has invested the relationship with her coach with elements that can sink a productive student-teacher relationship. The teacher has become a parent, for example. The student has abandoned her responsibility for her actions, even for the effort to work at improving. She has made herself into a child again and expects her good mommy/teacher will do everything for her.

I was taken by Pete Sampras's description, in various interviews, of how difficult it was for him to break with his coach and mentor. The time finally came, Sampras said, when he didn't feel the man could help him any longer, but still the break was very difficult for him to make.

I wonder if Sampras knew that he had every right to change, indeed owed it to himself to do so, when he thought it was appropriate. In the end, of course, he did change his coach and his learning environment, and with it effected some wonderful changes in his game and career.

Ideally, there should be enough maturity in any relationship between a student and a teacher so that each can be caring and supportive, but each can also sustain his or her own identity. They can then be honest with each other as the relationship evolves. Then, if a serious problem starts to develop, it will not be a surprise to either person. They both will know it, talk about it, and reach adult decisions.

Indeed, with a good coach, the idea of separating might very well come from her. "I'm not so sure I can help you here," she might say, acknowledging that you have changed as a player during the time you two have worked together and now you will benefit more from a coach with a different style and different goals.

Growth of this sort is natural. Yet I hear of so many coaches who try to sign up young players to ten-year, even lifetime contracts, a terrible arrangement for the student. Such a contract, a form of bondage actually, will restrict that child's professional growth terribly. It will prevent her from moving to a new coach, if her normal development requires it.

Coaches don't own students, young or old; coaches give lessons when students want them and are willing to pay for them.

Choosing and Changing Doubles Partners

When people think about matching themselves with a partner, usually they measure the ways their own tennis skills will complement those of the other player.

That's the easy and less important part.

Much more important is psychological compatibility, and it applies to several aspects of any doubles team.

To start with, when you're thinking about a partner, think about ending the relationship.

That might seem like an odd early priority — after all,

you haven't even played a match together — but let's examine it.

For a doubles team to work, the partners must be able to talk to each other and share relevant feelings. From that perspective, then, how do you see your prospective partner? Is this a person with whom you would expect an easy, open relationship so that if you reached a point where playing together was no longer fun, you could simply say so, and both of you could go your separate ways?

That's the feeling you want toward a new partner, and you should be able to talk to him or her at the very beginning in those terms. This is not a marriage. This is a relationship on a tennis court that should increase the pleasure you both find in the game. And when that pleasure turns to aggravation, it's time for each of you to find another partner.

That should be part of your first conversation, and that understanding should inform your partnership. If it does, it will remove the kind of tension that commonly develops between partners at those times when their play drops off. Then, without such an understanding, both players feel trapped.

In addition, look for a partner who is psychologically compatible with you in at least three ways.

- First, you want the kind of person who, like yourself, pushes herself to make her best effort throughout every match, even if her play is off, or you two are clearly overmatched.

  Otherwise, you will find yourself chasing down every ball, as always, while she doesn't even move for a lob. That will be tremendously frustrating and irritating.
- Second, select a person who talks to you.

  Avoid strong silent types. There should be a regular flow between the two of you. Some of it will concern the game, your strategy, which opponent to hit to. Some of it should be more personal, how each of you is feeling. Watch a good doubles team. After nearly every point they have their heads together, whispering, plotting the next point, giving each other support.

Another reason you want someone who can talk to you is that you don't want to be surprised by her behavior. There are enough surprises in the course of the normal match. You don't want a partner who starts going berserk in the middle of a match, or turns surly and angry with no warning. If this is a dreadful day, she should be able to tell you before you get on the court, and perhaps you both can agree that trying to focus on the match will be therapeutic. You don't want to feel that in addition to the team on the other side of the net, you also have to play against your partner.

- Third, find a partner who is automatically supportive of your play.

You are certainly going to have days when your play is off. When that happens, you want a partner who immediately begins to take more balls down the middle and starts telling you, "Don't worry. Just keep playing. You'll get back on your game."

You want a person who is strong enough to respond to your problem in a healthy way, not someone who is going to be disturbed by your play, who starts snipping: "God, can't you get one service return back? . . . I mean, that's five overheads in a row you've missed."

If you hear that kind of thing from her, end the partnership. It's not worth continuing. You can tell her: "I'm not comfortable any longer when we play. Somehow we're just not meshing. I think new partners will be better for both of us."

If there is reasonable psychological compatibility between partners, they will both be able to recognize problems in the partnership should they start to develop.

Like the mature relationship between student and coach I noted earlier, there will be no surprises over such fractures.

If you find yourself confronting such a situation and your partner won't discuss it with you, that's your cue to get out of the relationship.

I was surprised not long ago to read a statement from Rick Leach that he heard that his partner Jim Pugh had said their relationship was going "stale." They were at one time the best doubles team in the world. They subsequently split. What surprised me, if the report was true, was that two partners who could play as long and as well as they did together were not expressing such strong, important feelings directly to each other.

All too often, doubles teams stay together, even though the players are not playing well as a team and/or they are growing in different ways. But, neither player knows how to say, "It will be better for both of us to find new partners."

Nor can one speak honestly with the other for fear of hurting his feelings. If you break up your doubles partnership, you don't have to condemn your partner for anything. You can remain friends off the court. But unless you tell the truth, you are going to pay a price down the road, anyway.

Splitting can be tough. When Martina Navratilova split with Pam Shriver after many successful years and championships as a team, Pam spoke of the difficulty of the separation. It came at a time when she was trying to come back from injuries and a drop in her career. But she responded like the strong intelligent woman she is. In 1991, she teamed with Natalia Zvereva, a powerful doubles player who won the Wimbledon doubles title that year, and together they took the U.S. Open title in three sets.

It was a heartening, meaningful victory for Pam. Among those who shared in her pleasure was Martina, who happily and correctly noted that obviously what Pam had needed at that point in her life was a new doubles partner.

And obviously they both subsequently decided that each had now reached a point where they were ready to play together again; in 1992, they were winning tournaments together once more.

/ PART III

Playing Mental Tennis

CHAPTER 9

A New Kind of Winning: You Can't Lose

AT THE TENNIS COLLEGE, I meet a fair number of people who say they are not interested in competing. They maintain that when they play tennis, winning doesn't matter to them. Many of these people play a pretty fair game, so their attitude is not a rationalization for limited skills. In fact, even though they are not playing to win, they want to improve their skills, or they probably wouldn't be at the Tennis College. Their reasons for not competing are, I suspect, reasonably complicated and deep within them.

Competition is a demon of our society. It can warp athletics, learning, and life for children. It can pervert work, love, and life for adults. Later in this chapter, we'll consider some of those damaging effects.

Yet, while I believe that, I also believe there is a healthy kind of competition. And in my view, most people who eliminate competition from tennis are denying themselves one of the pleasures of the game. When they rule out competition, they are ruling out the excitement of taking a risk, the exhilarating feeling you experience when you are testing yourself and you are scared.

We don't have a lot of opportunities in life that provide us such excitement. A win-lose situation is decisive, black and white. Most of us live lives that are gray.

Most people spend their working lives in jobs that require them to be extremely codependent on others.

Until recently, one of my three daughters had been making video commercials at an advertising agency. At a gathering shortly before she left, one of her bosses told me that he was delighted to be retiring soon. The advertising business had changed a great deal for the worse, he said. Most agencies, he explained, now put vast numbers of people into the planning process of a campaign, so that no one person can be blamed if it fails (an approach that is, I think, common to countless businesses these days). But at the same time, if the campaign works, no single person can fully experience the joy of success. To be sure, that does not prevent everyone from claiming the success. Still, the reward is an empty one.

But when you compete, you are out there performing on your own. No one is going to hit that crucial backhand passing shot for you. If you can do it, and hit it correctly, even if you don't win the point, the effort and the intent will be so rewarding, you will feel that it is good to be alive.

Furthermore, while competing in tennis does involve taking a chance, it is a risk with a safety net. At work, where you could lose your job, the risk might not be worth it. But to lose a point or a match should be of little significance. So, there would seem to be much to gain by competing in tennis, little to lose. (At least for most of us. As we have seen, a loss on the court can affect some people as powerfully as if it were the loss of a job.)

According to the rules, you're supposed to try to beat your opponent, and if you're honest about it, to beat your opponent as fully as you can. You are supposed to play the best you can and also to be a decent person as you do so. That's how tennis is conceived and constructed.

The nature of the sport, when you think about it, challenges you to create a strategy that will enable you to penetrate an opponent's weakness. If you're playing against a person who is overweight and slow, for example, you should run that person all over the court. Doing so is not being cruel to your fellow human being (assuming you don't taunt your opponent). That is how the game is supposed to be played. An awful lot of people, however, would feel guilt over such a strategy, so instead, they'd keep hitting to their opponent on the baseline, letting him stand there and whack his powerful forehand.

The late Bill Veeck, former owner of the Chicago White Sox, had only one leg, but he was a pretty good tennis player. He used to get furious at people who patted the ball back to him. He wanted to play. He wasn't out there for sympathy.

An important aspect of smart mental tennis is analyzing an opponent's strengths and weaknesses, then crafting a game that exploits his weaknesses. What psychological problems would you have in "outsmarting" an opponent? A good player, for example, might gamble and serve to his opponent's strong side on a critical point because he knows that if he can win that point off his opponent's strength, he will undermine his opponent's confidence.

Does that sound devious and dirty to you? It's not.

I'm talking about competing and winning as a result of your effort and your skill. I am not talking about playing to win at all costs, which, sadly, an awful lot of people do. They will abuse their opponents, manipulate them, and, of course, cheat. They will do anything to win.

I saw a coach recently working with junior players. Every time one of the children called a ball that was close to the line "out," he cheered them. "Now you're playing the pro way," he shouted. "When it's close, call it out."

What he was really teaching those children was to win at the expense of other people, that winning justifies everything. People who pursue that philosophy might win a few more matches, but they pay a terrible internal price.

Among professional tennis players, this is sometimes obvious, sometimes not. It might be reflected in dreadful personal relationships, or self-destructive actions, or in explosive behavior after the match, of which I've seen quite a lot. Not long ago, an Australian champ destroyed a hotel room with his racket, smashing furniture, mirrors, everything because he lost a match. He had placed so much emphasis on winning a tennis match that the loss had shattered his self-esteem.

Or, to carry the meaning of winning perhaps to its ultimate, I read a small survey of weight lifters and other athletes who were asked before the 1984 Olympics, "What would you choose: You could win the Olympics by taking drugs, but have only ten years to live, versus not winning and living until you were seventy or eighty?"

An unbelievable number chose winning the Olympics and dying in ten years.

That doesn't sound like a very good deal to me, but it is a reflection of the place that winning has in much of our culture. I want to examine that a bit. Because in order to compete the healthy way, in order to try and win in the way I am advocating, you have to reexamine the meaning of winning in your life.

If you do, you might allow yourself to compete in ways so that you cannot lose.

Creating the Win-Win Condition

Probably the most important goal I can point you toward is to put yourself always in a win-win situation.

Certainly I hope that by the end of this book you understand this idea clearly enough so that every time you play tennis you will be in that situation. Perhaps the idea will mean enough to you that you can apply it to life beyond the tennis courts as well.

Win-win is an essential antidote to the manic stress in our culture on winning at all costs. As I said, when it comes to tennis or any sport, I believe in competing healthily, in trying to win. But that does not mean that I see the game only in terms of winning or losing.

Actually, I see it as a win-win proposition.

To achieve this in tennis, start with the idea that when you are out there on the court, it is not winning the match on the scoreboard that matters most. What matters most are other elements much closer and more meaningful to you as an individual.

What matters more, for example, is that you make every effort to execute each stroke properly.

That you play every point as well as you can.

If you do that, then you have done the very best that your brain and your body can do. Once you have done that, you are in a win-win situation. No matter what the score, you win.

Arthur Ashe told me that all the great players he had known had gone through a stage in their lives when hitting the ball properly on critical points meant more to them than winning or losing.

That's what I'm talking about. Do your very best. Play your hardest. Focus on that. That becomes your goal, not ending up with more points than your opponent.

If you do that, how can you lose?

Achieving it is completely up to you. It is all in your mind. If you commit yourself to playing that way, it doesn't matter what your opponent does.

Your opponent can be Jim Courier. He might bash one ace after another past you. Or hit the most murderous forehands at you when you go to the net, with so much power they knock the racket right out of your hand. It doesn't matter. You're still playing the very best you know how. And that is your goal. If along the way you also happen to beat Jim Courier, well, terrific! By all means, call everybody you know and tell them. But, if you don't beat Jim Courier, you still don't lose in the deeper meaning of that word. You have won. You have played your match.

Furthermore, along the way, you will have improved. If, in fact, you are able to go out and hit each ball properly, your game is going to improve. I guarantee that.

In order to achieve a win-win state, you have to rise above the win-lose mentality that is hammered into most of us as we grow up playing sports. Let me give you an example I have seen over and over again.

One player goes out and plays a match against another whom she has never beaten. The first player concentrates hard, focuses on each stroke, plays the best match she has ever played. But she loses.

She walks off and she says, "Can you believe it, I lost to Francine again. Number two thousand three hundred and thirty-three in a row."

What that poor woman doesn't recognize is that she has executed better than she ever has in her life. But because of her win-lose mentality, she cannot even see and enjoy her real accomplishment, her real win.

Tennis is not about winning and losing in the usual terms.

Tennis is about creating win-win situations, and savoring them.

Because of the dreadful win-lose mentality we are all inflicted with, people cannot give themselves credit unless they win the match in the traditional way, 6–4, 7–5. Even if they play badly, commit 100 unforced errors, and win only because their opponent commits 150, they still pride themselves in having won on the scoreboard.

If they lose, on the other hand, nothing else matters: that they made the right strokes, tried their best, did everything even though conditions were lousy, they were tired, the sun was hot, they were sunburned.

When I see people play that way, the last thing I care

about is if they lost the match love and love. If they played as fully as they can, then they really made gains. Then they won.

We all have to exorcise from our minds all the destructive cultural win-lose conditioning and doctrine.

When you play a match at your very best level, whatever the score ends up being, you have won and you should toast yourself. You deserve a gold medal. You deserve a cup. Something on the order of the cup they award at Wimbledon. Maybe a tad smaller.

Let me share a story about a four-time Wimbledon champion, Rod Laver, that I think wonderfully illustrates what I mean.

In 1975, Laver was playing Cliff Richey in Lakeway, Texas, just outside Austin, in a rather special match. At the time, Richey was number one in the world. Rod was past his prime, though still playing quite a bit and trying to regain the number-one position. He and I and Michael Davies, who was Executive Director of World Championship Tennis, had just finished making a film appropriately called *Just Once More for the Rocket*, and this match seemed to be his last shot at it.

In the first set, Richey beat Rocket, and in the second he had a pretty big lead. I was doing the telecast with Don Drysdale, the former great pitcher with the Dodgers who did a good deal of television sports broadcasting. At one point, off-camera, Don said to me, "Well, it looks like a wrap."

"Don't be so certain," I said to him. "It doesn't matter to Rocket what the score is. He hits the ball the way it has to be hit no matter what the score is. So he's always in the match."

Sure enough, Rocket started to move and he won the second set. So it was one set each and now they were playing the third and final set. Richey moved ahead again, 5–2. But Rocket kept hitting the ball just the way he had to hit it. At no time in that third set did Rocket have any self-fulfilling self-doubts, or did he get discouraged and say, "That's the end of this." He played the match shot by shot, concentrating totally on his own game.

Down 5–2 in the third set, he kept hitting and kept playing and finally tied it 5–5. In those days they played 9-point tiebreakers. It went to 4–4 with Richey serving. In the stands, people were going crazy. They were so happy for Rocket because he was fighting back. He had been so far down in the second set, it looked as if it was all over, then he came back. In the third set, he had been down again, and he came back and tied it up. Does the old guy have it in him to come back and beat the number-one player in the world? The place was going crazy.

So, Richey served and Rocket murdered it. Absolutely murdered it. Richey, off-balance, dove for it and just managed to get his racket on it. The ball plopped over the net. Richey sat there. He had won the match.

Well, people in the stands were crying. They were beside themselves with pain for Rocket. He had hit the perfect shot in this return of serve, the shot that would have given him the match, the shot that might have turned his whole career around. But with a desperate lunge, Richey had won it. The place went gaga.

Frankly, I didn't know quite what to say to Laver, but I had to interview him after the match. So I said, "Well, Rocket, *I'm* at something of a loss. How do *you* feel?"

"I feel great, Vic!" he said. "We're going fishing. There's a place not far from here and there are fabulous fish, they're running now, and we're going this afternoon!"

I looked at him. "Yes, but Rocket, how do you feel about the match?"

"Well, Vic, didn't you see the last play? I nailed that sucker!"

In his mind, he hit the shot that he had to hit. And in his

mind he said, "If I hit that shot a hundred times, I'm going to win ninety-nine of those times. Richey knows it. I know it. If a guy dives for the ball and it plops over the net, there's nothing I can do about that."

I realized why he was so great. He hit the shot, he did his very best. He felt pride. And now, he was going to reward himself. He was going out and have a great time fishing.

In a way, that's what I want for all my students at the Tennis College and I hope for every tennis player reading this book.

Try to hit the ball, to execute properly.

And then reward yourself for that effort.

If you can put yourself in that situation and approach tennis that way, you're in a win-win situation. Rod Laver's attitude in that match is a great example of a win-win mentality. In his mind, he won because he hit the right shot and he hit it wonderfully.

Imagine that for a moment, from a man who has won every major championship in the world. He won the Grand Slam, the four greatest tournaments in the world: Australian Open, French Open, Wimbledon, and the U.S. Open. He won all four in one year and he did it in two different years. So he knows what it is to win. He knows what points mean. He didn't win this big point, and yet in his mind, he lost nothing.

If you can grasp that idea, and carry it onto the court, you can never lose.

Savor the Golden No-Win Opportunity

There is a variation of the win-win situation that can also enrich your tennis. It's the no-win situation, but not the no-win situation you're accustomed to hearing about in which life is hopeless. Quite the contrary.

In this one, this kind of match, you have no realistic chance of winning in the traditional 6–1, 6–2 sense. Your opponent is simply far too good.

But that can become a golden opportunity for you, if you can approach it with the right attitude, if you can acknowledge that you have nothing to lose, and therefore, loosen up and play your best tennis with absolute impunity.

There was a wonderful example of this at Wimbledon in 1985 that reflects both sides of the no-win condition, the effects of the must-win pressure on the favorite and the effects of the removal of pressure on the underdog.

In the early rounds, Kevin Curren beat Jimmy Connors and John McEnroe. He aced Connors thirty-three times. Curren has an extremely hard, fast serve and it was working beautifully for him. And even though he had several career wins over top players, nobody picked him or even assumed he had a chance to reach the finals, where he ended up against Boris Becker.

Now, in the earlier rounds against Connors and McEnroe, Curren had everything to gain and nothing to lose. If he won, it would be an upset. If he lost, it would be no disgrace. That placed Curren in the golden no-win position, free to hit and hit and hit. He was liberated.

Most people watching that sort of match don't understand the nature of that pressure. But it is the reason why a lot of very young players win big matches. Tracy Austin beat Martina Navratilova at age fifteen and Chris Evert at age sixteen. In her autobiography, *Beyond Center Court,* Tracy said that she could see the pressure on their faces even before the matches began. Of the time when she was only fourteen and playing Chris at Wimbledon, she wrote, "I felt no pressure. I had nothing to lose. In fact I was more nervous about curtsying to the royal box than about playing. . . ." Meanwhile, as Chris wrote of that match in her own autobiography, *Chrissie,* she got sick to her stomach before it started.

It happens over and over again. Most recently, of course, we've seen Jennifer Capriati do the same thing. She was completely loose. In her first year as a pro, who could expect anything of a fourteen-year-old, and one with such a nice smile? Nobody favored her for anything. She simply had to go out and play as well as she could. No pressure on her. It was up to Steffi and Gabriela and Martina and all the rest of them to beat her. Indeed, they were expected to beat her.

It was the same for Curren in the early rounds. Once he got to the finals, however, he was the favorite. Now he was expected to win and it changed his whole mental set. Playing against a seventeen-year-old kid, Boris Becker, having beaten just days before two of the best players in the entire world, Curren had a special kind of pressure upon him, and an enormous amount of it.

As I watched him, I suspected rather quickly that he was going to lose. The key was in the way he nervously moved his head and glanced over at Becker before he struck the ball on his serve.

When he did that he was playing in what the motor-learning people call the "conscious state." In other words, he was pressing, trying to coach himself as he played. He knew what he had to do to serve against Becker, and he should have simply gone with that unconscious knowledge. His conscious effort interfered with what he knew, and with the natural flow of his serve. He was no longer the regular Kevin Curren. Now he was Kevin Curren, the Wimbledon favorite.

That glance, which was a result of all the pressure, distorted his normal movements and varied the position of his racket. On a flat serve, tests show, you can tolerate a variation of ½ to 1 degree. Curren, with his pressure twitch, was exceeding that, and the results were catastrophic. His serve was off, and without his biggest weapon, the rest of his game collapsed.

On paper, at that time, Curren had a better serve than

Becker, but that was all he had that was better. Becker was much more solid off the ground. So, without the big serve, Curren had little chance.

Going into the match, people expected Kevin to win — and it's reasonable to assume that he did too, given the way he was playing, the press he was getting, what everyone was telling him. But there was a considerable gap between that expectation and the reality of Boris Becker's enormously strong game.

In the end, of course, the pressure and the reality of Becker's game were more than Curren could handle, and he lost in four sets. If he had been able to shuck the psychological baggage, however, he might have had a chance, though he still had the problem of strokes. A healthy mental attitude alone will not win you a Wimbledon title. You still need the strokes and the game to go with that attitude, and Kevin's game was limited. He still played well enough during those two weeks to reach a point that only a handful of all tennis players ever reach, and he has played fine matches since. But his big chance for a lifetime of fame escaped him.

All of this does not mean that if a player finds himself in the position of being the favorite, he is doomed to lose. Not at all. But that player has to deal with the attendant pressure.

After Wimbledon, Becker himself commented that he went into the match feeling he had everything to win, nothing to lose. When life deals you that hand, play it with relish.

If You Take Gas

Winning and losing affect us differently.

The best players go onto the court thinking they will win. It's hard for them not to imagine themselves winning; they don't go into a match with self-doubts. If they are playing someone who might be ranked slightly higher, they know they will be in for a tough match, but they are not fearful of the other player. They are fixed on what they have to do in order to beat that player.

Once they have eliminated the whole question of losing, they are free to concentrate completely on their own strengths and strokes and strategies. They are able to exclude external factors that could play on their minds, undermine their confidence, and upset their game.

But you can count on one hand the players — no matter how great they are — who at some point in their life don't have to deal with defeat. Normally, of course, this comes most meaningfully in the last year or two of a career when the player is simply slowing down a bit or losing the transcendent edge that players at the very top must have.

Whatever the reason for the change, it does come. People start to beat them. We have seen that, of course, in recent years with such spectacular champions as Chris Evert, Martina Navratilova, Jimmy Connors, and John McEnroe.

There was one champion I knew, Alex Olmedo, who coped with losses in a way that offers something of a healthy lesson.

As an amateur back in the days before there was open tennis, Alex was a great champion. He beat Rod Laver in straight sets to win Wimbledon in 1959, the same year he got to the finals of the U.S. Championships. He was a Davis Cup star, winning two singles matches and doubles in 1958, when to everyone's amazement the United States upset the Australian champions.

Soon after that, Alex turned pro for what was then a lot of money, and began to play on the pro level. He was considered one of the best players in the world, and coming off his tremendous Davis Cup triumph, he was a national tennis hero.

In the pros, he lost by my count nineteen straight matches. Nineteen consecutive nights, Gonzales and the others murdered him. In one way, Alex was victimized by the form of

pro tennis in those days. The tour consisted of the four sup-
posedly best players in the world. Alex was a great champion,
but he was up against greater champions, Rosewall, Pancho
Segura, and Gonzales, night after night. He did not have the
opportunity he would today of playing in a field of sixty-four,
a different tournament week after week. He would have
flourished in such a professional system and become a mul-
timillionaire. Instead, it was as if he had to play against
Connors, Courier, and Edberg, each in his prime, night
after night. That was Alex's fate, and he could not win a
match.

Try to imagine that. How do you handle it? What's the
effect of it?

For Alex, it was a terrible blow, no question about that.
Even though, finally, he started to win again, he never suc-
ceeded much on the tour.

But to his credit, he was able to face this totally surprising
defeat. He realized that while he would never be the champion he was before, it was not the end of the world. A
delightful man, Alex became an extremely popular teaching
pro in Beverly Hills, and has always made a comfortable living from tennis, teaching at the Beverly Hills Hotel and elsewhere.

He was able to keep this sudden turn in perspective. At
the time that happens, at the time you lose or have a string
of losses, it can be quite disturbing. It's especially tough if
this is what you do professionally, if this is how you earn your
living. Then a good deal of your personality, the value you
place on yourself, is tied up in what's happening.

After all, one of the ways that people define themselves
and their value is by the work they do and the quality of that
work. If they produce shoddy work, they will not have high
feelings about themselves. If they produce work they are
proud of, they will feel better about themselves. For Alex, in
that sense, it was a profound disturbance.

The rest of us, however, are not among the top ten tennis players in the world. Our perspective should take that into account. If you enter a tournament and there are, say, sixty-four people in it, sixty-three of you are going to take gas.

So, you should be prepared for two possibilities:

1. the possibility of taking gas;
2. the possibility that there is life after gas.

CHAPTER 10

Five Elements of Success

IN THE LAST CHAPTER , we considered competing and winning in the context of improving yourself and your tennis game. In a sense, this is what this whole book is about: how you can reach your fullest potential and experience your greatest pleasure.

In this grand pursuit, there are five elements I have observed over the years that largely define how well any player can perform: genetics, physics and engineering, psychology, experience, and conditioning.

They are reality checks, suggesting realistic guidelines and limits. Not that I want to discourage anyone from stretching, but at the same time, unrealistic expectations only lead to frustration and neurotic behavior. Rollo May, a brilliant psychiatrist, observed that anxiety takes place when there is a cleavage between expectation and reality. The greater the discrepancy between expectations and reality, the greater the chances for disturbed behavior.

Genetics

Braden's Natural Law #1: All people are not created equal for tennis, alas, but often you can compensate.

Years ago, among my pleasant fantasies, I saw myself as a

professional basketball player. In fact, I was not a bad player by any means, loved the sport, even coached it. But I am 5'7" tall with a four-inch vertical jump. Today in the NBA, except for point guards, anyone under 6'8" is practically too short.

Height is a genetic predisposition for serious basketball. In tennis, height does not matter so much, fortunately for me, as well as champions like Rod Laver (5'8½") and Ken Rosewall (5'7").

Tennis is really a game of position and balance, of being able to move, of speed. But, even if you are not blessed with certain natural advantages, like speed, there are equalizers, especially among average players. For example, if your genes provided you with a good set of eyes and fast hands, they can compensate at a club level of play, which covers most of us, for that missing foot speed.

There are, however, myths about height as a great advantage on the serve and at the net, as if a player who is, say, 6'5" can hammer a serve down. He can't. If he recruits muscles to hit down, rather than hitting off the natural arc of the racket, the racket will face down too much and the ball will not go over the net. With all the tall tournament players we've monitored with electromyography, not one recruited muscles to hit down on the ball.

Tests by Dr. Howard Brody of the University of Pennsylvania, one of tennis's foremost physicists, show that if your racket reaches eight feet in the air, normal for anyone who is around 5'7", and you hit it with no spin at 100 miles per hour, an extremely good speed, then the following happens: if your racket is 5 degrees past vertical, when you strike the ball, it goes long; if it is 5.5 degrees past vertical, the ball goes in the box; if it is 6 degrees past vertical, the ball goes into the net.

At 100 miles per hour, then, you are playing with only half a degree of space. If you are, say, 6'10", you might have a bit more space than half a degree, but not enough to make a great difference.

Beyond which, once that 6'10" player hits his serve, he's got to contend with the return of serve, and if he's playing against a fairly good player, that return is going to come back at his feet, a very difficult shot for an extremely tall person.

Wilt Chamberlain serving might look awesome, which could certainly give him an advantage, unless his opponent knows enough to focus on the ball and not on the specter of a giant swinging. Wilt Chamberlain at the net might appear unpassable, but try a simple, deep lob. True, if you try to pass him and your passing shot is weak, he's got extra inches that might matter. But even then, what matters more is whether Wilt has the reflexes to take that first, critical step to the ball quickly.

It is speed that matters so much more than height in tennis. It certainly can be the difference between good players and great ones. This becomes even truer today when new rackets allow players to speed the ball up.

The best players today are extremely fast. I mentioned Michael Chang and his remarkable ability to race to balls that would be winners against slower players. Watching Edberg beat Jim Courier in three straight sets in the finals of the 1991 U.S. Open was dazzling in many ways, most especially Edberg's speed and agility. At times he seemed to be at the net before his serve had landed on the other side.

Edberg combines his speed with anticipation, a lethal combination for any player. He was not only at the net in the blink of an eye, he was waiting for Courier's return of serve as if he were reading Courier's mind.

In fact, if you are not as fast as you would like to be, you can compensate to some degree by anticipating shots, which we discussed earlier in the book.

Physics and Engineering

I lump these two together as one element in this analysis of success because they are so intertwined in *Braden's Natural*

*Law #2: The player who comes closest to honoring the desired phys-
ical laws is normally the winner.*

What I mean here begins with an observation that few
players ever make: tennis is played on a long, narrow sidewalk. The singles court is 27 feet wide by 78 feet in length.
For doubles, add 4.5 feet for each alley, so you now have a
court 36 feet wide.

From one corner to another on the singles court is only
19.1 degrees. Visualize that, or draw the angle on a piece of
paper. It's not much, is it? It expands to 24.2 degrees from
one corner to another in doubles, but that is a very tough
shot.

If you look at tennis this way, you see that you don't have
much room. It is easy to hit a 30-degree shot, but then you
would be 5 degrees off.

If you begin to think, "I am a prisoner on a long narrow
sidewalk," you can cut down on your wide shots.

That the court is only 78 feet long raises a related problem
of physics: how easy it is to hit a ball well yet send it far
beyond the length of the court, especially with the extra
power of the new rackets. In many ways, they are wonderful,
but they cannot help you if you point one of them wrong.
Then you hit the ball with more power and it goes farther
out of bounds.

These new rackets are also lighter. If you now play with
a 10-ounce racket instead of the one you had that was
12 ounces, you can whip it and roll it that much faster. That
might make you feel good, but in terms of physics, your
chances of mishitting the ball increase.

There is no question that the new rackets require you to
be more careful than ever to develop good strokes.

Considering the physical laws related to the width
and length of a tennis court, it is no wonder that tennis
has spawned so many racketball players. Countless tennis players found that in racketball they didn't have to
be nearly so precise. They could mishit the ball, yet still

bounce it off the side wall and remain in the point.

In the previous chapter, I spoke of the problems that Kevin Curren experienced in the finals at Wimbledon of 1985. The pressure he felt affected his serve and his forehand as well, which, as he hits it, is a difficult shot that requires considerable racket play. Physics intervened. He had about 15/1000ths of a second to roll his racket face. His muscles could not respond the way they did when he played without pressure.

I think we've been seeing the same battle recently between physical laws and John McEnroe. He also has a forehand and wonderful "quick hand" shots that require precise and delicate timing. But he's getting older and he cannot honor the physical laws that require him to be inside 15 milliseconds on some of his shots.

Unless the laws of physics are honored, unless you have the proper engineering in your shots, you are not going to enjoy much success in tennis. I've had countless players come to me saying they needed psychological help to improve their games. Needless to say, I responded to such a plea. Yet, in every single case, as soon as I took a look at them on the court it was clear that their problem was strokes. Their engineering was off. And not surprisingly, once we corrected that, their psychological problems often vanished.

Psychology

Braden's Natural Law #3: Providing opponents have equal ability, the player who can block out all undesirable psychological factors is normally the winner.

Throughout the book, we've been discussing psychological effects on your game. The variety is vast. What they share is their impact on the brain, which in turn affects muscle responses.

The result can determine whether you win or lose a match. Think about the times you go onto the court carrying with you anger from the office. Or the burden of a feud with your spouse. Or guilt for taking time out of the day to indulge yourself in an hour of tennis.

It doesn't take very much. Constantly in pro tennis you hear a player mutter: "I lost my concentration for one minute and, *bang!* I was out of the match."

In this regard, Chris Evert made an interesting comparison recently between Monica Seles and Jennifer Capriati. "With Monica," she said, "you can see it in her eyes. She is relentless and never seems to lose concentration. But Capriati has a tendency to lose it, to float away for a while, and that gets costly for her."

Psychological attitude is critical. I mentioned Edberg earlier recovering confidence in his game after he was able to fight through a period of lost confidence and beat Chang. It wasn't simply that he beat a difficult opponent. What mattered was the way he processed the win internally. Edberg recognized that he had been abandoning fights. This time, he stayed firm. As a result, he demonstrated to himself that he had the inner qualities to win tough matches. After that, he started to play with a new ease and confidence.

What makes Boris Becker so unpredictable? Why does his game swing to such extreme heights and then flatten out so? Players on the tour speak of him as the best in the world, if he is playing with the right attitude, if he is attuned to the match, if indeed on any given day he feels like playing.

Sound familiar?

Experience

Braden's Natural Law #4: The player who has been in a number of tight match situations and has learned how to use that experience effectively is normally the winner.

For that player, the win-lose moment is not foreign. It is not loaded with potential surprises, fraught with the anxieties of the unknown. He can maintain his equilibrium and focus on the factors that are important. The best of players under these circumstances are able to isolate the moment from the emotion of the situation. Rod Laver knew just what he had to do with Cliff Richey's serve, whether or not it was one of the most critical points in his whole career.

Why is it that some people love to get into tiebreakers, while others practically faint when they reach that point?

You can be fairly sure that the player who smiles comfortably is one who has been there many times before and won a number of them. He has, in other words, shown himself that there is nothing special to fear even though the pressure is increased.

Also, he has probably proved to himself that under such pressure, he is still capable of hitting the ball properly. He will not choke on that backhand which has been working so well for two hours, and now try to play it safe. No, he will hit it the way he has been hitting it, the muscles will be recruited in the same effective way. He might even have grown to enjoy the pressure.

If you find that you have played countless tiebreakers, yet almost never win, remember that experience alone is not sufficient. What matters is the experience of trying to hit the right shot, win or lose, under those circumstances. You do not gain anything if you repeat the same destructive pattern, if, for example, you try to put every shot away (as if to end the agony quickly).

But if you can try to play the point as if it were just another point, remembering that the ball does not know how close this match is, and try to honor the laws of physics, then you will create a breakthrough for yourself. You will show yourself that you can play that way. And you will show yourself that that is the only way to play.

Conditioning

Braden's Natural Law #5: Provided both players have equal ability and experience, honor physical laws, and maintain sound psychological attitudes, then the better-conditioned player normally wins.

I'm sure you recognize the truth of this when you think of matches of your own. What happens to you in the third set? Are you still moving well, concentrating sharply on the shot? Or are you no longer getting to shots you were putting away an hour earlier? Are you standing there flat-footed and facing the net, not even moving your feet or getting into position to hit the ball correctly?

At the club level, the importance of conditioning is often demonstrated quite dramatically. Look for it the next time you watch a match. One person is playing pretty much the way he did in the first set, making some errors, but trying to hit the ball properly, trying to follow his game plan. The other is fighting to stay alert.

Jimmy Connors was inspirational at the U.S. Open in 1991, and his resilience and stamina gave new hope to middle-aged players. But earlier in the year, in the French Open, when he was coming back to the tour after injuries, he wasn't yet in good shape. In the third round against Michael Chang, he managed to carry himself into the fifth set, but then he had to stop. His back was acting up. His body was running down. He defaulted.

In Chapter 12, we'll consider ways to exercise and condition yourself. The truth is that if the old body cannot respond, not all the ability, experience, respect of physical laws, and healthy mental state in the world are going to help.

In fact, that formula applies to each of the five qualities I've been discussing in this chapter. You need them all. If one is missing, your efficiency will decrease considerably. If you are psychologically sound out there on the court, for example, but weak on physics, I'm afraid you are destined to be a happy loser.

CHAPTER 11

Your Game Is Only
as Good as Your Data

WE ALL GATHER DATA by simply looking around and seeing. But very often in tennis and other sports, what we think we see is not what is actually happening. So, we receive data, but it is not very accurate.

Good data, on the other hand, is the reality of what is happening to the ball, to you, to your opponent — the reality as opposed to what you imagine is happening.

It is frequently so different from your perceptions, it can stun you. Certainly, it has had that effect on countless numbers of my students. But if you can apply good data to your game, it can dramatically affect the way you approach and play tennis.

Poor information, meanwhile, blocks you from improving your game.

After a number of studies in both our tennis and skiing colleges, we found three predominant reasons why people did not improve.

The first and most important: They had poor information.

Beyond that, information had not been provided to them in ways that matched their learning-system preferences.

And third, their own fears and anxieties impeded them.

Inaccurate data can affect your play in extremely fundamental ways — in how you hit (or mishit) topspin, for example, or in how high you should try to hit the ball over the net. Inaccurate data is at the root of the most common serve problems, serves based on the scratch-your-back theory of serving. Inaccurate data is also at the root of a widespread overhead problem.

Let's examine these and other ways your game is profoundly affected by what you think you see, bearing in mind that what you see is not what you get.

Deceiving Appearances

Most critical movements in sports are faster than the human eye can record accurately.

When you watched Bjorn Borg play, you were especially aware of his powerful topspin ground strokes. When you watched him hit the ball, you saw him bring his racket over the ball in a fairly dramatic, exaggerated motion, going from very low to very high.

Seeing that, it was quite natural to assume that it was his exaggerated low-to-high swing with the racket rolling over the top of the ball that imparted his enormous topspin to the ball.

Borg affected countless club players. They saw Borg play and tried to do the same thing with their own forehands. But when they did it, the ball spun quickly into the ground. Needless to say, they were puzzled.

What their naked eye could not see was what was really happening when Borg hit the ball. I was able to pick it up with high-speed film, which I could slow down and play frame by frame.

It showed that Borg hit with a vertical racket face, the racket moving from low to high. His arm went through the ball and toward the intended target, and only long after he had made contact with the ball did his forearm roll over, a movement that made it appear as if his racket were rolling over the ball. The key to it all was that his racket head was vertical and never rolled over the ball at all at the time of impact.

It happened so fast, however, it looked as if he were rolling the racket over the ball in the middle of the stroke.

Borg's power came from another movement that most viewers missed, if for another reason.

People commonly said that Borg stood facing the net. Contrary to what their coaches were constantly reminding them — turn sideways to the net — the number-one tennis player in the world was simply standing there, facing the net, yet smacking the ball with such power that opposing players at the net had their rackets rattled.

As an awful lot of club players interpreted that, it provided a wonderful excuse to be lazy and not take the extra steps to prepare for a shot by turning sideways.

Actually, Borg prepared for each shot by massively rotating the top of his body away from the net. He turned nearly 100 degrees more with his upper body than the normal player who turns sideways to the net. The average player turns about 20 degrees. Borg's feet faced the net, yet often his opponent could see the back side of the shoulder on the nonhitting side. To do that, as you'll see for yourself if you try it, you must turn at least 120 degrees. It was one reason Borg could hit his forehand so hard.

Most people missed this key move because while Borg was coiling himself, they were watching the ball and his opponent as he hit it on the other side of the net. They followed the ball back toward Borg, by which point he was uncoiling his upper body, lashing into the ball with his huge looping low-to-high stroke. So, what many saw was his body facing the net.

This compound misperception produced compound errors. Players planted themselves facing the net and tried to hit topspin by snapping their forearms and bringing their rackets over the top of the ball. If you face the net and do not coil your body like Borg did, or Agassi does today, you are hitting with your arm alone, without the benefit of your body. Do that and you will not generate any power to speak of, and you will eventually strain your arm. Add to that the result I mentioned earlier, and you end up with a weak shot that drops a few feet in front of you, at most.

Not what you had in mind, perhaps, but what you had in mind was created by faulty data.

Let's look at another illusion in tennis.

Going back a few years, if you asked intelligent tennis fans whether Chris Evert or Martina Navratilova had the more powerful ground strokes, the great majority would answer, "Martina, of course. What kind of question is that?"

But the truth is that Chris Evert had much more power in her ground strokes than Martina. The difference was that Martina *looked* much stronger than Chrissy. But as anyone who has ever played against both of them would tell you, Chrissy's ground strokes, especially her backhand, were deeper and faster than Martina's, although Martina hit the ball hard and certainly had other aspects of her game that more than compensated.

How High over the Net?

When the best players hit the ball, how high over the net does it go?

How high should it go when you hit it?

Here we have a wonderful example of how what you see is not what you get, with far-reaching effects.

I've done various studies on this, and as part of one of them I asked a number of people at a match in Los Angeles, "How high do you think the following players hit over the net when they hit deep ground strokes: Borg, Connors, and McEnroe?"

People gave me predictable answers. "Well," they said, "Borg would be up to about four or five feet over the net. Connors, of course, hits a very flat shot. He would probably be about six inches over the net. McEnroe may be a foot to two feet over the net."

So we shot high-speed film during this tournament and it confirmed what we knew. When Jimmy Connors hit a deep shot, his ball was not six inches over the net, even though it might look that way to someone in the stands. His ball was about *three to four feet* over the net.

McEnroe was about *four to six feet* over the net.

And Borg was about *six to ten feet* over the net. Borg's ball, in fact, was so high it kept going out of the top of the frame. We had to reset our camera in order to keep it in range.

These are average figures, and they varied depending on the kind of spin a player put on a particular shot. But the point, I think, is fairly clear.

Separately, we monitored Chris Evert's shots and we learned that most of them went from four to seven feet above the net. Gabriela Sabatini's shots go higher than that, so the ball bounces even higher, providing tremendous topspin. That makes her difficult and tiring to play against. Borg's very high trajectories were so tough to play against that he won Wimbledon five years in a row.

Physicist Howard Brody provided me with interesting data on this. If you hit a ground stroke about waist-high, which is to say, three feet off the ground, from a spot three feet behind the baseline, the ball coming off your racket at 18 degrees with five revolutions per second of topspin — very little — and you hit it at a speed of 50 miles per hour, the speed of a good club player's forehand, that ball will go over the middle of the net 9.54 feet in the air, which is 6.54 feet over the three-foot-high net. It will land 75.54 feet in the court, which is 78 feet long.

This and other data that I gleaned from filming Connors, McEnroe, and Borg clearly tell us that most players need to hit the ball much higher over the net than they ever imagined.

Still, what's fascinating to me is that roughly 99.99 percent of the tennis population think that if they can learn to hit low, flat balls, they'll win.

The Great Flat-Shot Myth

There is a widespread fallacy about hitting flat shots.

So many players think that they are hitting well if they can get the ball over the net, hard and low. I constantly see people misuse ball machines this way, proudly bashing one net-skimmer after another.

But the low net-skimming shot normally produces easy balls for an opponent, unless she is volleying at the net.

Simple physics seal your fate: your shot is going to fall short, providing your opponent with a lovely put-away, or at the least a splendid approach shot and opportunity to move to the net.

Look at the data. Let's say you are playing at sea level at the baseline, which is 39 feet away from the net, and your ball is six inches higher than the net when you strike it. In order for that ball to go over the net and land near your opponent's baseline, you have to hit it, according to the best estimates of physicists and engineers, somewhere between 165 and 212 miles per hour.

As a point of reference, Boris Becker can serve at only about 120 miles an hour.

Yet we get people all the time saying, "I like to play flat. I don't like your idea of hitting the stroke from low to high. I really like it flat."

"Okay," I tell them, "but then you've got to hit it close to 200 miles an hour. That's pretty fast."

Steffi Graf, who hits what is probably the hardest baseline forehand in the history of women's tennis, reaches a little under 80 miles an hour, sometimes.

As I said, people don't realize this is a lifting game.

If you are playing at sea level and hit the ball with mild rotating topspin around 45 miles per hour, the speed of a B club player's forehand, in order to have that ball go the full length of the court, 78 feet, you must hit it about six feet over the net.

Six feet over the net surprises an awful lot of people. "If I hit the ball that high," they invariably say, "it would go over the mountain."

The problem for most people, however, is not that they hit too long, but that they hit too short. And with short balls, their opponents come in and beat them up.

Getting the ball over the net will not make you a winner, if you barely get it over. If you hit it less than four feet over the net, you are going to be in trouble because that ball will land inside the service line most of the time.

My studies show that the easiest ball to return for beginners, intermediates, and advanced players — which pretty well covers everyone — is a hard line drive, a net-skimmer that lands in the middle of the court and bounces waist-high. A much, much tougher shot to return is one with a high trajectory.

This is all simple physics: the gravity parabola, the arcing route the ball is forced by gravity to follow. The ball you hit will describe a certain parabola. It must go high enough above the net so that when gravity brings it down, it will fall at the point where you want it to fall on the court. Try it during your next practice session.

If you can factor into your game the idea of hitting higher over the net, you will improve your tennis dramatically.

And you can do that by following one of the real secrets to winning in tennis: Aim for imaginary target areas above the net.

This applies to all shots. It doesn't matter whether you're hitting underspin, topspin, or whatever. Aim for a window above the net that's in your mind's eye. If you make the ball go through that window, it will land at your desired target.

At our tennis college, we have roped windows at different heights that students try to hit through. The windows make it easier to identify the height at which you want the ball to pass over the net. I hear that more and more professionals around the country are using devices of this sort. But if you don't have one, ask a friend to stand at the net and hold a racket way up over his or her head. You hit over the top of it. That will begin to give you a sense of where you want to be hitting.

Or tie balloons to the net and let them float at different heights. Hit your favorite shot at one of the balloons and observe where the ball lands.

Or set out targets on the baseline and try to hit them. As you begin to do so, note the height at which your ball is passing over the net. Your brain will store that information and you will begin to create the software package you need to achieve that height automatically.

Keep gravity in mind. Each ball you hit is on a gravity parabola. If you know how high to hit it, it will land where you want it to land, where gravity forces it to land. If you're having trouble doing this, remember where your friend was at the net, visualize him, and recall how you had to hit over his racket before you could hit a deep ball.

Tennis is a lifting game.

You lift the ball up over the net to create the parabola you need. That's why you've got to know where your window is. Then, break that window.

The Physics of Spin

One of the great flat-ball myths is that Jack Kramer hit only a very flat ball. But no matter what it looked like, Jack hit with both underspin and topspin.

In fact, it is very hard to hit a flat ball. I once did a demonstration with physicist Patrick Keating showing that most courts themselves put so much topspin on the ball that when you return a typical waist-high shot by swinging upward 17-degrees with a vertical racket face, the ball goes back with little or no spin. In other words, most shots require more than a 17-degree lift to hit with topspin, more like 30 to 35 degrees, and at least 17 degrees to counteract the court's effect and end up with no spin.

Unless you are volleying, then, every ball you hit on a typical court has topspin on it. Even when a ball has underspin, it's going to hit the court and end up with topspin. It will have less topspin, but it will have topspin. That means you are really trying to hit a ball against topspin. Even if your opponent is slicing heavily, you must try to lift it.

Underspin coming at you, especially on high backhand shots, is easier to return with more underspin. When you hit it back with underspin, the ball continues rotating in the same manner as before it hit your racket. You don't have to reverse it. So, in some ways, because of the physics involved, underspin is easier to return.

Scientists talk about the Magnus Effect on a sphere. What it means for tennis is that when you swing from low to high and strike the ball with a vertical racket face, you produce topspin, a force on the ball that causes it to follow a dramatic arc downward.

Struck in the opposite manner, the ball carries with underspin, moving on a more horizontal line without the dramatic dropping arc.

With underspin, you don't have to recruit as many muscles and put so much effort into the ball to hit a deep shot. The problem, however, is that you cannot hit a short crosscourt underspin shot hard because of its tendency to float. That's why the hard hitters like Becker or Agassi or Courier are largely topspin hitters. They can absolutely blast the ball, but the turbulence their topspin creates on top of the ball forces their shots to drop in.

This information is useful if you play against someone who hits only underspin backhands. An underspin backhand can be hit hard down the line, a 78-foot shot. But if hit short, it can't be hit too hard or it will float out of the court. So when you go to the net against one of these players, try to make them hit crosscourt, in other words, toward the opposite service box. That's 65 feet, 9 inches. But underspin has a tendency to travel 70 feet on almost all fully stroked shots. So if you force an opponent hitting an underspin backhand into an area that is 65 feet, 9 inches, 99.9 percent of the time that shot will be 4 feet, 3 inches out.

The numbers and the physics might not exactly become part of your software, but the uses of topspin as opposed to underspin, and when to call upon each, can be significant to your game.

Use topspin . . .

1. *When you want to drive hard.* Because it forces the ball downward after clearing the net, use it like the big bashers in the pros for power.
2. *For passing shots.* It's especially effective on long passing shots down the line as well as short angled crosscourt passing shots.

3. *To wear down your opponent.* Topspin can cause your ball to bounce higher and render shots difficult and tiring for opponents.

4. *To lob.* It's good for offensive lobs as a way of surprising opponents. That is, however, a difficult shot and requires practice.

5. *Against an attacking opponent.* Your topspin return to a volleyer's feet can force him to hit his shot defensively, popping it up to you.

6. *To force your opponent's returns.* Since topspin shots can be hit harder, they reduce the time an opponent has to get into position for his shot.

Use underspin . . .

1. *For steadiness.* Underspin offers a nice way to hit steady, conservative deep shots.

2. *To pace yourself.* Hitting underspin will save you energy.

3. *To change the pace.* Underspin allows you to take speed off the ball.

4. *To buy time.* Tactically, it can buy you more time to respond to the next shot.

The Worst Way to Hit a Serve

Let's take another example of how your eye tricks you and damages your tennis: the serve.

Many people who come to the Tennis College and ask for help on their serve have been taught to scratch their back with the racket.

The fact is that if you truly scratch your back, you are serving with far less efficiency than you might. And if you could see the best professionals serving on slowed-down film, frame by frame, you would see that they are not really scratching their backs, they are doing something else with their upper bodies: they are uncoiling their upper bodies in the manner that baseball pitchers uncoil.

Not many people know this, but the whole idea of scratching your back with your racket has nothing to do with serving. It has to do with sculpture.

Many years ago a rather famous player named Les Stoefen, Sr., modeled the serve position for a tennis trophy. As I heard the story, and verified it with his wife, Stoefen, to the sculptor's eye, did not look sufficiently interesting or dramatic, so he repositioned Stoefen's hands and racket.

The racket got pointed upward, while Les's hitting elbow dropped. The hand that tossed the ball was pointed skyward.

It might have looked good to the sculptor and become something of a teaching model, but it is nevertheless a terrible way to hit a serve.

It stops your swinging motion. If you stop your racket motion, all your built-up energy is lost and you must start all over again. That usually means a violent muscle recruitment as well as a slower serve. Or, put differently, the circular motion of the racket is broken, the racket stops when it touches your back, and in effect the entire swing must begin again.

In my fairly widespread research, shooting top players with high-speed film, we found only one who scratched the back, Gabriela Sabatini. When she did that (she has made adjustments since), her serve was clocked at only 50 to 70 mph, which meant she was often hitting ground strokes harder than her serve.

In fact, the best serves are actually made in a very different way, in the style of a baseball pitcher. That's because the large muscle groups in your upper body that turn and abruptly stop when you go through the motion of a baseball pitcher transfer energy to the next link in the serve (or pitching) process and provide power to your serve (or pitch). When you serve, the final link in the process is when you stop your elbow, and your forearm and hand in unison snap the racket as if it were a whip. With this technique, you can make that whip go very fast and your serve go very fast with a minimum amount of energy.

To be sure, there are some players, even at the highest levels, who serve the back-scratch way. But they do so, I am certain, because they were taught that way, continued that way, and now find it difficult to break out of that style.

That certainly happens. Sometimes very good players misread themselves. What they think they are doing is not what they are doing at all.

I had a number of conversations with Jimmy Connors about his serve and he always maintained that it had helped him enormously over the years, that it was unquestionably a great source of his strength. "Look at all the tournaments I've won with it," he'd invariably argue.

But the truth was, as any number of players told me, his serve was extremely vulnerable. It was his service return, among other powerful strokes, that provided his strength.

On videotape, you could see that Jimmy threw the ball far too high, and at the point when he generated maximum racket-head speed, there was no ball in his window yet to hit. So, he paused, used a little time dropping his upper body, then jumped off the ground before his hitting forearm had achieved its maximum speed. The result was a serve in the 75 mph range.

To his great credit, he has, at this late stage in his career, recently changed and greatly improved his serve, lowering his toss. Nevertheless, to me it is absolutely remarkable that Jimmy won Wimbledon, the U.S. Open, and so many tough tournaments without a big serve.

In fact, if Connors had possessed a big serve, he might have been the best man ever to play the game.

Women and the Serve Trap

For years, women were lousy servers, largely, I am convinced, because they tended to fall into a psychological trap that was in part reinforced by misperception.

They were convinced that they had to have muscles to hit the ball hard. But it isn't muscle that allows you to hit a serve hard, as we've learned through biomechanics, the study of human motion. Not muscle, but being biomechanically efficient — getting the greatest result with the least amount of energy expended.

When I think back on women who won championships, it's difficult to come up with one who had a hard, fast, powerful serve. Billie Jean King used her serve wisely, but it was not terribly fast. Though Rosie Casals could at times hit a hard serve, she relied more on spin than speed. And both, it's worth noting, were superb athletes. Françoise Durr, who was a Wimbledon semifinalist, and a high-ranking pro, had an absolutely helium serve.

I have a simple two-part explanation for this: First, these women were merely doing what they had been taught to do and what their coaches allowed them to do.

And, second, not unrelated, women at that time never threw balls very much and, therefore, hadn't developed the motion of a pitcher throwing a ball.

Then Title IX entered our school system. It mandated certain equality in the treatment of women when it came to school sports. One result was that more women learned for the first time how to throw a ball.

If you think back about thirty years, in a women's softball game, the woman playing third base might not even throw the ball directly to first base. She relayed it to the second basewoman, who in turn threw it to the first basewoman. By that time, the batter was on first base reading a newspaper.

But now, the barrier has been removed. Women are allowed and expected to play softball, for example, the same as men. They have learned how to throw a ball. So they throw to first like men do.

And increasingly, the motion of throwing the ball has been applied by women to the serve.

I've been accused of male chauvinism on this issue, but I think the opposite is true. If we look back thirty years, we see that most of the tennis coaches then were men, while most of the women served poorly, and that tells you something about those men.

Further, it is a fact that most educators and most female students did not care whether women threw a ball properly or not. Fortunately, when Title IX became effective in 1978, legions of female coaches were born. One result is that women are now taught to throw the way men are taught.

In 1983, Dr. Ariel and Dr. Ann Penny, my research associates, and I did some research on the throwing differences between the sexes.

We started with a 120-pound boy and a 120-pound girl. Each had been properly trained to throw a ball from shortstop to first base. The result was that at 120 pounds, the girl threw the ball at the same speed to first base as the boy. The major differences in throwing speed between sexes appeared as weight and height differences became pronounced.

As women began to throw better, as a group they began to serve better. Along with this, there was another breakthrough in tennis. First came World Team Tennis and then team tennis, both started by Billie Jean King. In my view, these have been among the best developments psychologically that could have happened for women.

Before team tennis, there were hardly any mixed doubles matches in major tournaments. In the 1940s and '50s, a few of the officials of major events like Wimbledon badgered male players into mixed doubles. But otherwise there was none.

Men dreaded mixed doubles. They got battered. Their male opponent would serve into their woman partner's backhand. And usually, she could not handle the serve. She popped the ball up, and the guy she was playing with got murdered on the volley return.

Then along came World Team Tennis and the two-handed backhand. Every night there were mixed-doubles matches, and they mattered. The guys were out there pounding serves at the women, and often the match between two teams came down to the last match, mixed doubles. Once again, implicit in team tennis was a new equality for women. They were not only allowed to play with men, they were given the freedom, if you will, to beat men, to bash a return of serve back to a man.

Furthermore, they were professionals. They were expected to play well. The attitudes of women playing in team tennis changed. They began to look at themselves as professional athletes with a match on the line. They worked at it. They worked at returning serve. Either they developed strong two-handed backhands, or they sweated in gyms to strengthen the forearm extensor muscles that are necessary for handling a hard serve on a one-hand backhand. And they started to return serves hard.

Through team tennis, I saw a dramatic improvement in women's serve and service return.

The Serve and Your Head

Let me make a point about the serve that you probably wouldn't pick up simply by watching servers.

You must keep your head and chest up when you serve.

Otherwise, you're probably going to change the face of

your racket, which will mean a loss of control over your serve.

Your head weighs more per inch than any other part of your body. If it moves down, it will be a powerful force downward. And frequently, when a player drops his head, he opens the face of his racket to compensate. That usually guarantees a misguided serve.

Another common head problem: looking out to see where you want to hit the serve, or you think the serve is going, before you actually hit it. That causes the head to jerk about.

I did a study once of John Newcombe, who had one of the most effective serves of modern times. I went on a ramp above the tennis court in Dallas where he was playing and set up the camera at the angle to which he was making his toss, to the right side of his head.

I wanted to see where his eyes would be when he served.

My camera was right in line with the ball and his eyes. At impact, his eyes were looking directly at the ball and into my camera lens. Just before his racket got up there to meet the ball, his eyes were there. First you saw his eyes, then you saw the ball. It demonstrates why he had a good serve. His head was very still and it was up.

Chris Evert made an interesting observation to me about this once on a plane trip. Keeping the head still, she said, was a characteristic common to all great athletes. They maintained a very still head when they were performing. It was true with golf. It was true with basketball. It certainly was true with tennis. It is also true with skiing: Your head and your upper body are still, if quietly active.

The Great Overhead Fallacy

On the basis of faulty data, on the basis of what they think they have seen good players do, average players carefully prepare for an overhead in a way designed to give them trouble.

Their first movement is to point a finger at the ball.

True, the pros often point a finger, but it is not the first thing they do. It is the third.

First, they coil their body.

Second, they move their nonhitting elbow upward toward the ball.

Third, they point that finger.

Fourth, they swing.

By pointing first, you lock your body. You cannot comfortably coil your body, if your arm is extended and your finger is pointing up toward the ball.

Instead, keep your eye on the ball and coil your body in preparation for the hit. Once your body is coiled, move your nonhitting elbow, pointing it up toward the ball. Only then, point your finger.

Now you are able to get tremendous power out of your overhead shot. You can uncoil your body and all your large muscle groups, and put all of that energy into the hit.

Also, when you hit the overhead, resist the common tendency to look and see where you've smashed the ball — before you've actually hit it.

In order to look, you pull that heavy head of yours down, and with that motion, you usually hit off-target.

Your head should stay up until you see your hitting arm pass your eyes. Once your arm passes your eyes, then it's too late for your head to do any damage.

Now You See It, Now You Don't

It will probably come as a considerable surprise to all tennis players, linesmen, referees, and fans when I say that no human eye is capable of accurately seeing where a tennis ball lands when it hits the court.

There are times, of course, when someone gets lucky, but as a general rule no one can see where the ball actually lands.

Am I saying that all the hawkeye players who argue that a ball they hit was inches inside the baseline 60, 70, 80 feet away from them, are in fact only guessing? Yes, I am saying that.

You might honestly believe that your crosscourt backhand topspin lob was the quintessential and perfect platonic defensive shot and it landed, appropriately, on the very outer edge of the baseline. You might honestly believe that, be willing to bet your family on it. But whether it was or not, is far beyond the powers of your eyes to determine.

Am I saying then, that when you, dear reader, of pure heart and transcendent honesty, call a shot hit by your best friend Roberta "just out," you may be cheating? Actually, yes. But once again, not intentionally so.

You call it the way you see it. The problem is the human eye is incapable of seeing what is actually happening because the ball is on the court about three milliseconds and the human eye does not accurately record a three-millisecond event.

From all of my testing, I found that the shot most often miscalled is the one that is on the line. It is almost always called out. It looks out to the caller. But in fact the ball has a tendency to roll as much as two inches, sometimes more on clay courts, before it takes off. The human eye, however, does not see that roll.

Your eye must make very rapid movements when the ball is coming into you, so your eye has a greater chance of making a mistake. There is further inaccuracy from eye displacement that occurs when your foot lands in the process of hitting a shot.

So, you measure from the ball's takeoff point. However, that is two inches away from its entry, its landing point. But since you and everyone else are unable to see the roll, many players call balls out that are in fact two inches in.

We end up with everyone guessing.

Further, contrary to what I had thought, all my tests reveal that the person with the worst perspective on judging the spot where a ball hits is usually the player. To make such a call, she requires critical vision, at the same time she is violently swinging the racket and jolting her body with running movements. They cause the eye to move enough to distort vision.

Next comes the umpire up in his chair. Given his sightlines and distance from the ball, he is in the second worst position for determining whether a ball is in or out.

According to my studies, the linesperson, who is sitting right on the line, was many times more accurate than the player or the umpire. Essentially the linesperson has twice as good a perspective on the ball as the umpire, even though the umpire can and does overrule the linesperson.

As for television replays, usually they are not worth much.

With a replay you get only 30 frames to your picture. The ball is on the court approximately 3/1000ths of a second. So with 30/1000ths you could miss any contact that the ball has with the court altogether. You can see a ball coming in and going out. If you freeze-frame every possible picture, you won't see the ball hitting the court unless you are lucky and the ball happened to come in contact with the court in one frame. Unlikely, but a television or still camera could catch the ball by accident right at the millisecond that it happens to hit the court.

As for a camera or a human eye seeing a ball actually on the strings, that is essentially impossible. Many photographers use a motor drive on their still cameras to shoot machine-gun style, hoping that they will catch a particular moment of ball-hitting-racket or player-hitting-ball, but it only happens if they are extremely lucky.

I know some photographers who have shot for years, and they are still trying. The ball is on the strings, as we have measured it over and over again, only four to six milliseconds. The normal motor-driven camera takes only five shots a second, which means it has 1/200th of a chance of getting a ball on the strings.

By extension, the idea of you, the player, visually following a ball onto your racket is hopeless.

I know that will come as something of a shock since you have been taught from the first day you ever took a tennis lesson, "Watch the ball hit your strings."

Doing that will help to keep your head down, but the truth is, that nobody, *nobody,* has ever seen the ball actually hit the strings.

Several ophthalmological researchers have reported that during the last part of the ball's flight onto your racket, it is traveling too fast for your eye to pan with it, and vision gets blurred to the point of absolute or legal blindness, 20/200.

When you are playing, even if you cherish the myth that you watch the ball carefully and keep your head down and your eye on that ball until the ball hits your strings, you are actually doing something very different.

As I noted earlier in the book, your brain made its decision about where, when, and how to hit the approaching ball long before it bounced. Your brain had to. If you make the decision after the ball has bounced, given the speed of the ball and how long it takes your brain to receive the message of the ball and recruit the muscles to hit it, you're going to be too late.

In most cases, you need about 200 milliseconds to recruit the muscles from the brain to effect the stroke. A minimum of 200. When the ball bounces, unless it's a very high ball, there are usually not 200 milliseconds left. That is why when the ball takes a bad hop, and you are playing it on the rise, you hardly ever return it. You do not have 200 milliseconds to recruit a new set of muscles. If you're following a ball onto the strings before making a decision, you're dead.

The same phenomenon applies to batters hitting balls from pitchers. As I said earlier, they often decide on whether or not to swing at a pitch on the basis of body cues they receive from the pitcher before he has released the ball, or at the latest before the ball is 18 feet from his hand. Otherwise, it is generally too late. And no one, not even my favorite, the phenomenal Ted Williams with his mythical supervision, could ever see the ball actually hit the bat. It is on there about three milliseconds.

Where Did That Ball Really Land?

We tested a great deal to gather data about the functioning of the human eye and brain in relation to the tennis ball.

We had people serve and we photographed the ball at high speed, thousands of frames, so that we were looking at milliseconds. There are a thousand milliseconds in one second. If you shoot a thousand frames a second, you can tell by counting the frames how long the ball is in contact with the court.

To measure where the ball landed, we created a kind of invisible ruler by marking very light little lines, 1/16th of an inch apart on the court. The camera could see them but the player could not, so they didn't distort his vision. This way, we could also measure how many sixteenths of an inch people were off on their calls, and measure how far a ball rolled on a shot.

We knew that a human being could not record a four-millisecond event. We also knew that the tennis ball was on the court about three milliseconds. That means that no human has ever seen a ball hit a court.

What you see instead is the image of a ball coming in and the image of a ball going out. And you interpolate. That's why when the line and the ball are extremely close, often you stall. You can't make the call because you've got so much input going to the brain.

When we started these tests, I thought that the player

himself would be the most accurate judge. We had good tournament players, and in one experiment we placed 110 people around the court calling the lines from 110 different places. Each, therefore, had a different perspective.

I wanted to see how much perspective mattered. We found that it certainly did. A person positioned at one point said the ball looked in to her. But a person watching the same ball from another part of the court thought it was way out. So where you are calling from is important.

I had each of the 110 people calling the lines keep a log of where the ball hit. Four or five people close to the court walked out with a stick and marked the spot on the court where they thought it hit. The rest noted measurements for each shot in their logs, four inches in, eight inches out and so on.

We made a number of interesting discoveries.

First, we were stunned to discover how far off on many serves the receiving player was.

We had that player put a mark with a special stick where he thought the serve landed. Then we compared that with the frame we had from our high-speed film and camera to see where the ball actually hit.

It was common for the player receiving the ball to be six to twelve inches off on the call, depending on how much body movement he had to make for his return. He had no doubt in his own mind that he saw the ball and he saw exactly where it hit. But he couldn't, in fact, accurately tell whether it was six inches in the service court or six inches out.

When calls were missed, we discovered that in general the person sitting on the sidelines at the service line was two times more accurate than the person in the umpire's chair sitting at the net and above it, and four times more accurate than the player receiving the serve.

But no one was in a truly good position to call the ball. Which leads me to think that if people really want precision in calls, electronic line calling will be installed. Meanwhile, without it, the greatest accuracy would seemingly be achieved by having linespeople make their calls without being over-ruled by chair umpires, unless the linesperson's vision was blocked in some way.

We also learned that the player receiving the ball had even less accurate vision if he had to run and hit the ball.

I was a little puzzled by that, but I shared my data with Dr. Bernie Slatt, a scientific researcher and author of the book *Hitting Blind*. He had put special sensors on the eyeballs of tennis players and he found that when a person runs, his vision goes from 20/20 to 20/200. 20/200 is a level of legal blindness. That meant that when a player runs and hits the ball, at that moment he could go and register as legally blind.

Other researchers have found that over the last 5.5 feet in which the ball passes the human eye, it moves so fast that the rapid eye movement necessary to trace it renders the hitter almost totally blind, momentarily.

In our tests, we also demonstrated how you can affect and manipulate the judgment of people calling the lines, of which many players have been accused.

At one point when we had 110 people out there calling shots, I said to them, "You know, what intrigues me is that you folks are actually very accurate." In truth, except for the person sitting right on the line, they were very inaccurate. (I was lying to them as part of the experiment, and after the project I admitted that I had been lying.) Then I went on to say to them, "I'm fascinated that you're all about four inches too short in your calls. I can't quite explain that, but just keep calling them the way you see them. That's the most impor-tant thing."

Guess what happened? Most of them added four inches to their calls. If they thought a ball was two inches out, they said six inches. It gives you a sense of the potential for manipulating linespeople.

In light of all this surprising data, what happens then to you, dear reader, a totally honest person?

"Roberta and I play every Thursday," you say. "How can we call them if we can't see them?"

The answer is you cheat a lot. Not intentionally. But you give people bad calls.

There is one rule I can give you. Nearly every ball that looked slightly out with our experiments was actually in.

So if you want peace of mind, give your opponent the benefit of the doubt. If the ball looks slightly out, it's probably in. Call it in.

Unfortunately, most people do the reverse: when in doubt, they call it out.

/ CHAPTER 12

Mental Practice

IN THE LAST CHAPTER, we considered good data, much of which I'm sure surprised you. And we looked at how you might improve your game, if you factor that data into your playing.

Let's keep those principles in mind as we look at the most fruitful ways to practice. There is no progress without practice. The catch is, it must be the right kind of practice. And that means the continued application of good data.

Practicing in the abstract, without specific goals and without the right mental perspective, is boring. Which is one good reason why people tend to practice so little and/or badly.

One common difficulty is the myth-of-Sisyphus problem. When it comes to practice, to improvement through tough work, we start thinking of ourselves like Sisyphus, the poor soul who was condemned by the gods to push a great boulder up a mountain. Every time he approached the summit, the rock slid down and he had to start all over again.

Albert Camus, the brilliant French philosopher and writer, used that myth as a metaphor for life's struggle. As he noted, "The gods thought with some reason that there is no more dreadful punishment than futile and hopeless labor."

That's a reasonable description of the way many of us feel out on the practice court. Improvement is simply too tough. Just when you seem to achieve some consistency with your backhand, you begin to realize that your volley needs a lot of work. Soon you're saying to yourself: "I've got a thousand things to change in my game before it gets any good. . . . I'm going to have to play ten years before I beat my friend Sam."

But good data tells us otherwise.

All It Takes Is One Change

When it comes to improvement, most players start thinking in terms of thousands of changes, and of course the whole idea becomes overwhelming.

But in fact, frequently all you have to do is solve one or two problems and you become a whole new tennis player.

Think about that: If you straighten out one single stroke, you can improve your game enormously.

That is true for C players and world champions alike. At one point, Jack Kramer was going to give up tennis because of the problems he was having with his backhand. He was only sixteen years old then, demonstrating all kinds of talent, but he was not winning in the juniors as much as he expected.

A man named Roche offered Jack help. Roche was an engineer, not a tennis coach. He had watched Kramer play and he had analyzed Kramer's backhand problems as a good engineer would. So far as Roche was concerned, Kramer had a mechanical problem and Roche devised a specific engineering solution for it. It was really very simple.

The following year, Jack Kramer became the youngest American ever to play in a Davis Cup challenge round. He had not solved five thousand problems. He had solved one.

Let's look at this from a different angle.

How many more balls do you think you have to return

each point to beat most of the people who now beat you in reasonably close matches?

The answer is one. You have to get your average up only one for most of the people you play.

That might not seem accurate or possible, but once again let me share some interesting data.

Actual Playing Time, Actual Number of Shots

Most people have the impression that a tennis match takes a long time. After all, they see or read about five-set matches in the pros that go three, four, even five hours. They have their own experiences playing in matches that may last only an hour, but certainly feel as if they have gone on for three or four.

That idea in your mind can greatly affect the way you practice, train, and condition. And it can affect your attitude when you go out to play a match.

But here's a surprising piece of information. I timed the actual playing time for a match between Andre Agassi and Paul Annacone that Agassi won, 6–4, 6–3.

The actual total amount of time that both players spent hitting the ball in the match was only 4.95 minutes. From the time the ball was served until the point was over was a total of only 4.95 minutes for two sets.

That broke down to 2.38 minutes in the first set and 2.57 minutes in the second.

A few other interesting and surprising statistics:

- The average hits per person per point in the first set was 1.65 shots. That's not even 2 shots by each person on each point.
- In the second set, it was 1.54 shots per person.

With that in mind, think about my advice: In order to improve your game and win more matches, all you have to do is return the ball one more time each point. Perhaps you can begin to see that if you are able to do that, you're going to start winning an awful lot more points.

I timed another match between Sabatini and Graf. Normally, of course, women have longer rallies than men. And in this match, they both played baseline games, though it is worth noting that in professional tennis, points are ended more quickly than in the average club match. Even so, the data is fascinating.

This was the finals of a tournament in Florida in 1989. Sabatini won it, 6–3, 4–6, 7–5. In other words, three long sets.

- The total number of hits in the match was 1,567 for those three sets.
- When you break it down to hits per person in the first set, it was an average of 3.8 hits per point, per person.
- In the second set it was 4.12 hits per point, per person.
- In the third set it was only 3.25 hits.

Think about what this means. With two of the steadiest players in women's professional tennis, somewhere between three and four hits by each player and the point is over.

Translate that to your game. Let's say that your present average is three hits per point. If you could get your average up one — to four hits — you have improved 33 percent.

Looked at another way, you're giving your opponent 33 percent more opportunities to lose.

Invariably, when I start to discuss this with students to help them develop a new attitude toward improving their own games, they say, "But look at the pros. They must hit twenty, thirty shots a point."

The research, however, shows otherwise. Here are Sabatini and Graf hitting 3.8 shots per person per point. So you don't need to worry about hitting another ten or twenty returns on a point. One more return than your opponent on a point will make an enormous difference in your game.

In support of this surprising data, our limited studies have found that if you get your average up one more ball back each point, and you played ten people who presently beat you in close matches, you could beat more than five of those people.

Mentally, most people identify with Sisyphus. They get it in their heads that in order to lift their game and begin to win, they have to develop unbelievable new shots, twists, spins, serves that haven't even been invented yet. Not so. You don't require anything unbelievable. The data show that all you've got to do is get one more ball back.

Think about that the next time you go out to practice. Just one more ball.

There is hope for all tennis players.

Being in Tennis Shape

Practicing intelligently and lifting your game by one more ball are going to be infinitely easier if you are in reasonable shape, and I refer to tennis shape.

I suspect that millions of tennis fans nearly fainted in recent years as commentators spoke of Agassi and others and their new conditioner, weight lifting. As if the rest of us didn't have enough to worry about transporting our own weight around a tennis court, now to win a few matches we've got to resemble Arnold Schwarzenegger.

But as I've already noted, body strength and awesome muscles will not determine a good tennis player. McEnroe and Connors, for example, have slight upper bodies. I remember when Dr. Ariel and I did a strength test on the great Pancho Segura, who hit one of the most fearsome forehands I've ever seen. His results on our strength machines

192 / Vic Braden's Mental Tennis

were so low, I had to check the machines; even children scored higher.

Yet Pancho's timing was so perfect on that forehand, and he used his body so well when he hit it, that he was a tremendously successful professional player.

As we've discussed, hitting with power is a matter of timing: of moving each link in the proper sequence with the proper timing, unleashing the maximum power into the ball through biomechanical efficiency.

For a splendid example, watch Pete Sampras hit a ground stroke. His front foot is well planted and his body moves so well from the ground up: his knees arrive first, then his hips, then his upper body, and then his arm. His timing is perfect.

You don't need an overabundance of muscle mass. Where the extra muscle helps Agassi and the others is when they hit and are off-balance, when they are late and lunging for a shot and all they've got is an arm sticking out.

Hitting from an off-balance position is common for all players, and that is when you can easily injure yourself.

I'm sure you can relate this to your own experience. People tell me: "I reached for a backhand, I was way out there, it hit the frame, and I felt my elbow go." That common injury might be prevented if the muscles protecting the elbow are built up.

Stretching exercises can also help you when you are in positions of special stress. If you include them in your practice plan, they will help when you land awkwardly and turn your ankle.

But if the idea of weight lifting and body building leaves you giggling, let me suggest a few simple alternatives.

Before undertaking any of these exercises, consult your physician. They might not be suitable for you and cause injury. You might also want to discuss them with a qualified exercise physiologist, who can lead you through the rationale of each resistive drill. If you undertake the exercises, do them slowly and without any sudden, jerking movements.

To protect yourself from tennis elbow

Tennis elbow is a painful injury that often comes from damaging backhand hits. But you can develop the supporting muscles you need quite easily.

Here's an exercise many tournament players swear by: Before you get on the court for a practice session, put your racket cover on your racket, and start swinging it as you would in a backhand stroke. The cover creates air resistance and that drag will strengthen your muscles.

Players tell me they usually do it until they feel a slight burning sensation. But don't overdo it.

The next step is to put a ball inside the cover and start swinging. You can increase the conditioning by adding another ball. You might even build up to the point where you can swing with three or four balls in the cover. But again, do not exceed your limits.

Protect yourself from damage to your Achilles' tendon

Do toe raises to stretch the Achilles' tendon, which joins the muscles in your calf to your heel bone. If you work out in a gym, this exercise will be even more effective if you can do it pushing up against a bar on your shoulders, or on a machine that provides you with that resistance.

Do these regularly, daily if possible, at least as part of every practice session and before every match.

I learned the importance of regularity with these toe lifts the painful way. About four years ago at UCLA, I was giving a clinic for some four hundred coaches, and talking about stretching as a preventive exercise. "For example, when you hit an overhead, you can land on your heel," I said. I leaped up to demonstrate my point, landed on my heel, and snapped my Achilles'. I hadn't been doing the exercises, so I provided the best demo of my life and was hobbled for weeks.

Build up your hamstrings

These are the muscles in the back of your thighs and knees. Tennis players tend to develop fairly strong quads, the big muscles in the front of the thighs, and the pros pay special attention to weight machines that build those bulging muscles. Certainly, they are important in a lifting game. But hamstring exercises get neglected, and hamstrings are what you need when you bend for low shots. Hamstring pulls are common. Again, if you use a gym, lie on your stomach and pull weights up with your legs.

Drink water

Before, during, and after each practice session, and certainly every match, drink lots of water. Dehydration sneaks up on your body, especially on hot days, and once you've reached a stage of liquid depletion, you cannot quickly catch up. A long drink of water at that moment will not be sufficient. Your body will be drained of energy, and you will have to stop playing and start replenishing your system with water. (Don't do what I see so many people doing, however, and drink from a plastic tennis can. There's wool and other residue from the tennis balls in those cans.)

In general, during practice or a match, observe the elements, especially heat and sun. The Aussies are accustomed to ferocious heat, and you see them wearing hats and playing with a wet handkerchief around the neck. Rod Laver used to put a piece of cabbage under his hat, which he insisted kept his head cool. Ivan Lendl learned from the Aussies. Now when he plays there, or in any tournament where the temperatures are punishing, he wears one of those Foreign Legion hats with a flap going back down his neck.

On hot days, when Jack Kramer was apt to get blisters on his feet because they slid around more, he used to apply Vaseline to the balls of his feet and wear three pairs of socks: a very thin pair and two pairs of wool socks. When he took that precaution, he wore tennis shoes that were half a size bigger than normal.

Do not run long distances

I'm sure you'll be pleased with this suggestion: Forget about marathons, at least so far as improving your tennis is concerned. If you have a passion for marathons, enjoy them. But they won't help you much in tennis.

Now and then, I read about a tennis player who runs ten or fifteen miles a day. That can be depressing. Even if you don't play tennis, that can be depressing.

But the fact is that the whole game of tennis is essentially a matter of taking only two or three steps.

The average number of steps to a ball is about three. '

Furthermore, there is increasing evidence that the first step is the critical one.

When you understand that, you must wonder about the usefulness and the intelligence of training for tennis by running ten to fifteen miles a day. Much more rewarding would be time spent practicing sprints, short-distance running, and simulating actual points.

Years ago, Rod Laver intuitively grasped this. At that time, Harry Hopman, the legendary Australian coach, required his players to run miles and miles a day. Laver tried it and his game actually suffered. Hopman, however, was a strict authoritarian and his system was not to be questioned.

Rod finally got his courage up, went to Hopman, and explained that the running was of no help. He improved his game, he told Hopman, by playing matches. Hopman heard him out, and to his credit and Laver's surprise, allowed Rod to alter his training regimen.

Not All Practice Helps

There is a cliché that practice makes perfect. But if you practice every shot the wrong way, you are not going to do much for yourself or your game. In fact, *perfect* practice makes perfect.

The best practice session is one that simulates playing conditions. If you loaf, floating about the court hitting a few strokes, you're wasting your time.

Jimmy Connors has a wonderful system. He goes all out for short bursts, working on specific strokes he wants to polish and hitting them just as hard as he would in a match. He runs just as hard too. His practice sessions are not long. He has had some of the best workouts I've ever seen, which lasted only twenty-five minutes. Yet, he worked so hard in those twenty-five minutes.

If you're practicing for matches that you expect to last sixty minutes, practice hard for seventy minutes. Get used to more than might be expected of you.

Above all, avoid practicing shots that don't exist in a match. Over and over I see people stand on the baseline and hit balls down the middle of the court to each other. In a match, your opponent normally tries to run you from one corner to another. Why not practice that way, hitting from corner to corner?

Or, with volleys, what good is it to stand at the net and have a friend pat a few putaways to you, when in a match your opponent is going to be hammering at you, forcing you to stretch and move all over the place?

Practice the Shots You Need Practice On . . .

Here's a very common habit: You have a problem with, say, your backhand. You're practicing, and the ball is hit to you down the middle of the court. What do you do? Instead of stepping into it with your faulty backhand, the stroke that needs attention and work, you inevitably step around it and hit a forehand.

Try to catch that and the related tendency we all have, which is to hide our flaws. The first step to improvement is to face a weakness and tell yourself that even if you have to look awkward, even if you have to spray balls all over adjoining courts, the only way you are going to develop a reasonable backhand is by possessing good information on what constitutes a good backhand and then practicing it.

Is HBO really televising this practice session live?

Practice is a special time when you are totally free to make mistakes and look your worst. Appreciate that. All performance pressures are off. If it is your backhand that needs work, that's all that matters. If anything, step around your forehand.

By the way, if you do step around a backhand when you're warming up to play in a match, you're telling your opponent that you don't like to hit backhands.

Quite purposefully, Jack Kramer used to hit the first warm-up ball right down the middle to an opponent in order to see which side the fellow stepped to for his return. His choice signaled to Jack the side his opponent preferred.

. . . Especially Serves . . .

People don't practice serves nearly enough.

Before you start a match, it's terribly important that you feel that your serve is right. When you warm up, hit at least ten serves in. And that means *in*. The best players in the world, the players on the pro tour, try to hit twenty serves in before they start a match.

Ken Rosewall would begin loosening his shoulder muscles long before he got onto the court, swinging slowly through perhaps a hundred serve motions. Yet I watch C players come out, hit two or three serves, and yell: "I think I've got it. . . . Okay, first ball in."

Having the right mental attitude about your serve is critical. I spoke of the importance of feeling comfortable with your serve and having confidence in it before you start the match. Hit ten in, hit twenty in. Try to sense an easy fluid motion on the serve. Swing slowly at first, so you can begin to feel the rhythm develop. Reach the point where you sense that your swing is smooth and natural, where you know that your body is working efficiently as you serve. It is the sequence of your body movements, their flow, and not violent muscle movements that creates the strong serve.

And, feel that when you hit a serve in, it is not because you are lucky, but because your motion is right, because you are hitting the ball on that serve exactly the way you want to hit it.

Also, remember to practice serves you are going to use in the match. Players come out and hit flat serves when they warm up, but in the match, they are constantly hitting a second serve with spin.

The two most important shots in tennis are the serve and the return of serve. Yet, those are the two shots that get practiced less than any other.

. . . And Return of Serve

One common way of practicing the serve is to take a bucket of balls out on the court and serve. Some people, however, don't like being out there all alone. There's a simple solution: Bring somebody with you. With two, one of you serves and the other returns. Then reverse it, so your arms don't get tired and there's variety in the practice session.

It's an excellent way to practice. Concentrate on the serve, just as you would in a match. You might hit ten to get into a groove, while your friend practices return of serve, then she hits ten serves.

Even better, rather than simply hitting, set up targets for each of you to aim for. In practice or a match, you always want to hit with a purpose.

If you don't practice your serve and return of serve, quite simply, your chances of losing increase.

Try the Superdrill in Your Head

One of the best practice drills I've ever seen comes from Dennis Ralston. His idea is to simulate a point, all by yourself, with no one on the other side of the net, and no ball.

You start with the serve. Even though you aren't actually hitting a ball, go through all the motions correctly: Keep your chin up as you're supposed to when you serve and try to hit that serve with the right form. Then move to the net, following in your imaginary serve. Take a split or check step, bring your feet up to a ready position just as you would on the court if you were coming in after your serve, to see which way your imaginary opponent is going to hit the service return. Then take off after that invisible ball.

Let's say you imagine a return that clears the net with topspin and drops quickly. That means you've got a low backhand volley. Run in and take the low backhand. Then, as you would on an actual point, move right on to the net. Run to the right. Take an imaginary forehand volley. Run back and hit an overhead.

In your mind, you might create an opponent who is immensely steady, keeps the ball in play, and runs you all over the court. Deep forehands, deep backhands; take a short ball; hit your approach shot. Keep moving, playing that tough point, until, finally, you win it.

You can perform all your shots perfectly, since there's no ball to distract you. So go through all the motions perfectly.

Bend your knees correctly, keep the racket head up on low volleys.

While you're bending down low, you're stretching your hamstrings and quads. Throughout this drill, your cardiovascular system is getting a great workout and you are using the exact muscles you would use in a match.

It's also helpful as a tool for visualizing the way points are played, which is especially good for net rushers. In that sense, it's rather like the exercise top ski racers put themselves through before a race, when they close their eyes and visualize the gates they'll have to go through.

You might even do Ralston's drill on the sidelines while you're waiting for a court. If you run one solid minute on this drill, you've used every muscle you can use in the match and you haven't even gotten to the court yet. In fact, one minute of this drill is roughly six times longer than the average real point. It's like playing six points, so be careful not to overdo it, and be sure to warm up sufficiently before you go through it.

It is a wonderful drill and it is tough. I remember once doing a video with Dennis Ralston in which he was to be our principal demonstrator. He went through his one-minute drill, and performed it expertly.

When it was over, the cameraman said to him, "Yeah, I like that. Let's do it." Dennis moaned. He, like all the rest of us, thought the cameras had been rolling. And even though he was at that time playing the pro tour and, of course, had been one of the best players in the world, he needed a break.

Stronger Second Serve Means Better First Serve

In Chapter 3, I mentioned the problem Stefan Edberg thought he had with his second serve. But once he saw the data on it, that his winning percentage with it was something like 80, he realized that he didn't have to worry about it at all.

One unanticipated immediate effect was that his first serve percentages improved. And you'll see that in your own game.

Practice that second serve. When your second serve reaches a level of dependability and efficiency where you know that you can continually depend on it, you will relieve a tremendous amount of stress about your serve. Consequently, your first serve will get better as well. And, once you become really efficient with your first serve, you can be very hard to beat.

At one point years ago when I was playing in some pro tournaments, Pancho Gonzales was beating everybody. He was fierce and intimidating and his first serve was so big and so effective, nobody could get near him. After a while, many of the pros said, "Hey, we've got to do something about this. He's got an unfair advantage."

You'll note that his opponents tended to blame Pancho for his achievement, rather than admitting that the real problem was ours, that we had to hit better service returns.

In Cleveland at that time, there was a tennis promoter named Jack March who agreed with Pancho's opponents and staged a one-ball-serve tournament. No more two serves. You hit one serve and that was it.

The idea behind it, of course, was that this would neutralize Pancho. There were twelve players in that tournament, six stars like Pancho, Frank Sedgman, and Pancho Segura, plus the journeymen like myself.

It was going to be the first one-ball-serve pro tournament, and everybody was very happy. They thought at last they were going to beat Gonzales, because they thought he was going to be serving second serves all the time. After all, they reasoned, if he's got only one serve, he's got to play it fairly safe.

Gonzales won that tournament faster than he had ever won any tournament. The reason was that everybody else was just as inefficient with the one serve as they had been with two. That meant that when Pancho was returning serve, it was usually a relatively weak one he could come in on and do with almost anything he wanted. Nobody had counted on that.

Further, nobody had figured that Pancho not only had a great first serve, but he had worked hard to develop that great first serve. It was no accident, no series of lucky shots. He had, indeed, developed a monstrous serve and he never expected to have to hit a second serve. He counted on his first serve going in, always. That was how he hit it.

As a result, in this screwball tournament, he still hit a big first serve and won all the points he normally would win with it, while all the other players were hitting their second serves which he could murder.

When you're effective, you're effective. And there's some evidence, at least in Pancho's case, that you don't lose that particular skill with age. I saw him play in a leukemia benefit in October 1992. He was sixty-four years old and his service motion was as beautifully fluid as ever.

Practicing with the Data

Pancho Segura was one of the best thinkers and strategists I've ever seen in the game, and one of the most underrated players in the history of tennis.

He was not a muscular man, as noted, and he also had leg problems. As a child in Ecuador, he had rickets and was told he would never be able to play any sport.

Largely by his intelligence and his courage, Pancho overcame adversity. He continually studied the game. And this was clearly reflected in the way he prepared for the first-ever

$10,000 tournament, in the late 1950s, an amount that astonished all of us on the pro tour.

Segura did well in the tournament at the L.A. Tennis Club and was to face Gonzales in the finals. The day before, I came across him at the club and I couldn't figure out what he was doing. He was out on the court all alone, bouncing the ball on his backhand side, hitting down-the-line shots, and then running diagonally across the court as fast as he could. I watched him for a while repeating that same drill, bouncing the ball and running, bouncing the ball and running, and finally I said, "Sneaky," — that's what we called him — "Sneaky, you okay? I mean, man, you look like you're on the sauce."

He turned around and smiled at me. "You know," he said, "Gorgo [Gonzales] has that continental hammerlock grip. So when I hit down the line and he has to stretch for his forehand volley, he can only go crosscourt with it, because of the way he holds the racket. . . ."

Segura was practicing what he expected to happen the next day in the finals. He figured that if he could run and get Gonzales's return, Gonzales would still be over by the alley, the whole court would be open, and he, Segura, could have an easy point.

This is a wonderful example of a player who extracted a single piece of data from a broader field of knowledge and used it to evolve a marvelous game plan.

Segura understood anatomical problems, in this case, problems related to the grip. He had analyzed that single piece of data, developed his game plan, and tested it.

Sure enough, on key points, Gonzales performed exactly as predicted. He took Segura's down-the-line passing shot and hit it crosscourt. Segura was there and he put the ball away.

Segura won the $10,000 tournament, largely off that shot.

Segura was also able to play the law of probability.

If you can predict with some accuracy how an opponent is going to hit a particular shot, say, eight out of ten times, that can shift the whole match to you. That knowledge can allow you to move as your opponent is hitting the ball, give you perhaps two more steps to get to the ball.

Breaking Habits

An increasing number of club players are using videos of themselves to study their own games. This is an immensely helpful tool that can show you aspects of your game you never imagined.

I should warn you, however, that if you use it, be prepared for an image shock. You might not look like what you imagine on the screen in your mind. It can be mildly upsetting when you are faced with, say, the visual evidence of your tummy.

Once you get over that, watch the video with your pro, or a pro who is good at video analysis, which all pros are not. One who is adept will be able to point out any number of important but subtle problems that you might otherwise overlook. Going frame by frame, she can show you an incorrect position of the arm, or a habit you have with excessive backswing on the forehand, and the angle of your racket for topspin — the kind of detail so meaningful for improvement.

You can also help yourself with a computer analysis of your game. CompuTennis is one such service. They come to your club, track you through a match, and provide you with a printout of your game: your second serve percentages, how many points you won on the backhand, how many points you won when you went to the forehand on the right side, how many points you won serving to your opponent's forehand. A ton of information.

In a simplified way, you can also gather data from an honest friend. Ask him about your weakest points. If he says, "I like to hit to your backhand deep in the corner because you look like you're choking," you have learned a lot about what to practice next.

One caution: Once you've extracted the data, by whatever technique, remember that making changes will not be easy. By all means, make the effort, but expect resistance from your inner self, from your established patterns and software. Changes can be difficult for all of us, with tennis or any skill.

We get accustomed to functioning in a certain way and psychologically that way becomes very comfortable for us. Whether it is efficient, productive, or not, it becomes comfortable.

If you try to change the way you hit a ball and you find yourself resisting and resisting, bear in mind that psychological comfort is a powerful quality for all of us. You might have to get a little uncomfortable before you can make the change you're after.

In my experience, people don't try to change unless they are dissatisfied with their play. They usually have to find themselves losing and in a crisis before they are sufficiently motivated.

Indeed, I would never ask anyone to change his game unless he came to me wanting to change. If players don't want it, their brain is not going to accept it anyway.

The world is full of frustrated coaches, some of whom have taken top-ten players and told them, "If you'd only do this, you'd be number one in the world." And the players don't do it because that's not how the human psyche works. That player's psyche says, "If I'm winning a lot, don't disturb it."

The big problem for that player comes when he decides he is indeed in serious trouble. A real crisis for a professional player can radically alter his fortunes, can mean a string of defeats that severely damages his earnings, his career, and, most important, his confidence.

So, at the point of crisis, he wants to change, and quickly. He then has the motivation to make a change. But it will not come overnight. It might not come at all, if his coach does not understand the physics of his game, or how new motor skills are learned.

Some years ago, Evelyn Ashford, the great sprinter, came to our sports research center with her coach Olga Connolly, the ex–Olympic champ.

Evelyn told me and Dr. Ariel that she was a natural runner, and in truth, she didn't even want to be at the center.

"Then why are you here?" Dr. Ariel asked her, a bit taken aback.

"Because my coach wants to understand what's happening when I run, so she can coach me better."

To me, both people were quite logical. Ashford did not want to tamper with anything, at least at that point. She was the world champion by doing whatever it was that she did, even if she didn't understand the process herself.

Her coach, however, was smart enough to know that if the day came when Evelyn needed to make a change, she, the coach, was going to have to possess sufficient knowledge of her runner's mechanics to change Ashford's software package, an intricate and delicate process. She also knew that the critical movements in Ashford's mechanics occurred faster than the human eye could register, a problem that could be dealt with by the three-dimensional analyses of Ashford's running that we were going to do that day.

Despite considerable psychological and physical discomfort, we regularly see examples of how the best tennis players continually change their games on the basis of good, new data.

Players often make fun of tennis scientists, but great champions are good scientists. They are always collecting, gathering, synthesizing data. They look at what works and, when something doesn't, they analyze why, and with new data, they adapt. This takes a huge effort on the practice court.

Jimmy Connors, for example, at the age of thirty-eight, changed his serve, and players tell me it is infinitely stronger.

As I said earlier, there were mechanical reasons for the problems or limitations with that serve. Connors finally accepted good data and changed. His toss is three feet lower and more to his powerful left side than it was five or six years ago. In those days, he never got to 80 miles an hour. Now, he can hit closer to 100 miles an hour.

Bjorn Borg made a similar adjustment about halfway through his career. As great as he was, he realized that he, too, could be more effective with a different serve. Think about that. You watch Bjorn Borg winning Wimbledon five years in a row and you say, "Not bad. I think I'd be pretty happy playing at that level." But Borg, like all great champions, was continually examining and analyzing his own game, continually trying to improve it.

He was not afraid to change, not so locked into habit or even success, that he could not change. He began throwing the ball lower and more to the right, not trying to hit such a big kick on his serve. He was after more speed and he got it. He began to serve it at 105, 110 miles an hour. Before, he was serving in the 80s.

Ivan Lendl has also made significant changes. After winning countless tournaments and grand slam championships, he looked at the data and said, "The data are clear. Unless I learn to volley, I cannot be number one in the world today." With tremendous dedication and months and months of effort, he learned to volley well.

A few years ago, Martina Navratilova, who had won every major women's title in the world, finally improved her forehand to the point where it could be a real weapon. Not many people even realized that she had only a mediocre forehand. But Martina knew it, and she knew exactly what it was costing her. She is a fierce worker, in addition to being a magnificent athlete, and she worked on that forehand for months. Finally, she began to see some results.

Even when she was firmly the number-one woman player in the world, she focused on another flaw, and developed a nice topspin backhand.

I remember broadcasting one match soon after. I had not seen her play for a while and after the match I said to her, "Martina, you have really done something with that backhand."

She smiled, and said, "Thanks, Vic, I'm glad somebody noticed."

/ CHAPTER 13

Mental on the Court

THROUGHOUT THIS BOOK, I've been analyzing tennis from the perspective of a coach who is also a psychologist, to provide you with an understanding of the game that may well be different from what you've had.

Along with that, I've been trying to show you how to reconstruct your game, shaping it around selected data.

While I've spoken theoretically, clearly my intention has been practical.

The test comes, of course, when you get out on the court.

My hope is that after reading this book, you will never play tennis in quite the same way again.

And that you will continually apply the observations, the advice, the data that are appropriate to your game, when you practice and when you play.

My hope is that you will never step out on the court again and simply hit the ball the way you've always hit it, make the same old mistakes all over again, and utter the same soft curses and prayers.

You now have available to you a new way to play tennis. You can be in control of your game.

It all comes together in a match. In this chapter, let's consider twelve specific pieces of data that should determine the way you play various shots and devise match strategies. If you program this data into your new mental tennis software, your responses to these common match situations will become automatic.

1. Return Crosscourt, Crosscourt

If you hit a slow, high crosscourt return, rather than a fast, low drive down the line, you can increase the time you have to move into position for the next shot by 300 percent.

I spoke earlier of working with the former Chinese champion Hu Na. She liked to return crosscourt shots low and hard down the line. It was a powerful shot, but she normally ended up with a short ball. That, plus the pace she put on the ball, gave her very little time to get into position for the next shot.

Then I showed her something with film and a stop-frame sequence analyzer. When she ran wide to return a crosscourt shot, we saw that she could give herself triple the time to get back into position on the court, if she hit a high crosscourt return rather than her hard down-the-line shot. Additionally, she gave her opponent a tougher ball to return.

Also, a ball hit crosscourt can travel 82.5 feet before it's out. If you hit it down the line, it has only 78 feet.

2. Another Caution on Down-the-Line Shots

If you take a deep crosscourt shot and go down the line with it rather than returning it crosscourt, studies show that you have an eight out of ten chance of losing that point.

This is important for your strategy, just as it is to any professional. Frequently, in pro tennis you see one person hit deep crosscourt to the other and the second player returns it deep crosscourt. The first player hits it back again deep crosscourt. The second player hits it back again deep crosscourt. And everybody in the stands is yelling, "Go down the line! Go down the line!"

But each of those players knows that the first person who takes a deep crosscourt shot and goes straight down the line has increased his chance of losing that point to eight out of ten.

Of course, if one of those players hits a short crosscourt ball, the other most certainly will pounce on it and then bang it down the line.

3. Save Steps

When the average tennis player hits a ball crosscourt, he or she will run all the way back to the middle of the court to prepare for the next shot.

The pros do not. They barely move two steps toward the center, even if they are way over in the corner of the court. That is because, as I said, they are fully aware of what the odds are if you take a crosscourt shot and try to return it down the line. They would be delighted to have their opponent try that.

They also know that if the player they are facing isn't a gambler, that player will return crosscourt anyway. So why should they go all the way back to the center of the court?

And they are aware of another advantage of the crosscourt shot: It can send an opponent chasing the ball into the alley, and beyond.

4. Pick Up Your Opponent's Body Cue on a Lob

In chapters 2 and 3, I spoke of the enormously important technique of picking up your opponent's bodily cues in order to anticipate shots. This is perhaps never easier than on a lob.

Whenever a player starts a forward movement into the ball, his or her muscles are committed.

When you see the average player drop a racket head, and it is coming straight up, you know it's going to be a lob. It's not going to be a drive. With that racket coming straight up, your opponent has committed herself. She does not have time to stop, send a new message to her brain to recruit new muscles in order to make a drive out of that shot.

So, respond immediately to a lob. That is the signal you have been given, and that is the message you want to send immediately to your brain.

As obvious as this seems, I watch countless players who can see that their opponent is going to hit a lob, who clearly receive that cue, yet they do not respond. They seem to be saying to themselves, "Well, I'm up at the net. She could be trying to trick me. She's really not going to lob." Even though their opponent is doing everything but yelling "This is a lob!," people stay there at the net and won't start moving back on the first cue.

5. Anticipating Down-the-Line Shots

People who are very late getting to the ball almost always go down the line with their shot. They have little choice because they are restricted physically: They cannot hit the ball far enough in front of their body to drive the ball crosscourt. So, they either go down the line or they lob.

Remember that, the next time you go to the net behind a nice approach shot deep and in the corner that forces your opponent to lurch wide and defensively for the ball.

6. Anticipating Drop Shots

You almost always see your opponent shorten his swing as he prepares to hit a drop shot. When you see that, start moving toward the net.

Also, begin to take notice that certain players will hit drop shots only on forehands. Or backhands. Or from a particular spot on the court.

The giveaway signals may not be quite so obvious when you play, say, Agassi. But against Lewis, your weekly opponent at the club, he might as well be attached to a fire alarm.

7. Flat Shot Means Short Shot

Any time you see an opponent on the baseline coming straight across the ball to hit a flat shot, start moving forward because that ball is probably going to fall inside the service line.

The data I mentioned earlier explain this: If a player is 39 feet away from the net standing on the baseline and hits a ball that is six inches higher than the net when he strokes it, in order to have it carry to the other baseline, he must hit it somewhere between 165 and 212 miles an hour. If he can hit a ball 200 miles an hour — and, to the best of my knowledge, no one ever has — then he can drive that flat ball from one baseline to another, in fact far beyond it. Otherwise, due to the laws of physics, the ball will drop short.

Be prepared.

8. Move Left with Your Opponent's Toss to the Left

If your opponent is an average right-handed player and serving to you, and he throws the ball far to the left of his body, you should be prepared to move to your left.

It is physically impossible for the server then to slice that ball or to hit a spin serve to your right.

The reverse is true for left-handed servers.

React this way, and you can run around your backhand and smack a forehand.

9. Move Right with Your Opponent's Toss to the Right

If that right-handed opponent throws it too far to the right, it will be difficult for him to hit it down the middle, and most players don't. When they throw it farther to the right than normal, they are usually signaling a slice. To be in the best position for that, break a little more to your right.

10. Strategies and Tactics: Applying Good Data, Ignoring Good Data

Your strategy for a match is your master plan. Your tactics allow you to implement the plan.

At times, a good player creates a game plan on the basis of a particular insight he has gleaned on another player. That is what Segura did against Gonzales.

That is also what Arthur Ashe did when he beat Jimmy Connors in the final at Wimbledon in 1975.

Arthur recognized that Jimmy was perfectly grooved from the baseline on waist-high and chest-high shots. But Jimmy was not strong on low balls to his forehand.

Arthur applied this intelligence, and his strategy for the match became forcing Jimmy to hit low forehands. His tactic was the chip shot. He began hitting the ball short, over and over again, and never gave Jimmy the kinds of shots he likes. He knew that Jimmy's stroke was not engineered for lower balls, especially lower balls that he had to hit while moving forward. So, Arthur hit short balls and lots of easy junky stuff and he won Wimbledon.

Arthur, who was a wonderful, rare, extremely intelligent man, was also capable of not recognizing data and making mistakes, though hardly ever twice. In the case I recall when he did, the data concerned drop shots.

In 1966, Rod Laver was playing Pancho Gonzales. Arthur,

Jack Kramer, and I were watching the match from the stands at the Sports Arena in Los Angeles.

At one point, Gonzales needed a point badly. He tried a drop shot, not Gonzales's type of shot at all. Laver easily got to the ball and put it away, to win that key point.

Jack turned and said, "Arthur, let that be a lesson to you. Never, ever drop shot when you need a point. Never."

I've never forgotten that. But Arthur, who normally played such intelligent tennis and got the most out of his own game, did.

The next year we were in Ecuador and Arthur was playing in the Davis Cup match in Guayaquil. He was down two sets to one, playing against Pancho Guzman, a man who had never taken a set from Arthur in his life. To be sure, Arthur was off his game. Stricken with some stomach ailment, he had been up all night vomiting. He had been undefeated in Davis Cup play, but lost his first match and now Ecuador led, 2–1. But Guzman was a player with no serve and clearly not in Arthur's class. Yet on clay in Guayaquil, he had Arthur down two sets to one.

In the locker room at the break, folks were screaming at Arthur and banging lockers because the United States was in danger of going down to defeat. Confusion reigned, yet it seemed clear to me that Arthur's strokes were so much better, he simply had to play his game and be patient. Mechanics win out every time.

The match continued and Arthur did not try anything fancy. He just played it straight. As a result, he won the fourth set 6–0. In the fifth set, Arthur went up two games to one and was about to go up three games to one. If he could do that, he'd win the set and the match.

Guzman was choking and serving at love–40. He hit a very soft serve, and on the return, Arthur tried a drop shot. Guzman got it and won the point. Arthur could have had a service break. But Guzman bounced back and, with the crowd roaring behind him, he didn't stop. Arthur lost the set, 6–3.

Even great champions make mistakes. Every great champion I know can recall all too vividly matches they would love to forget. However, great champions — and this certainly includes Arthur Ashe — do not have a record of repeating bad plays.

11. Not Adapting

It is easy to grow accustomed to playing your game, to play against an opponent in a certain way, and even though the data are terribly obvious, you don't acknowledge their message. You continue to play the way you always have.

There's a psychological comfort in sticking with what you know, in sticking with your game. But that can be costly, even for the best of players.

Guillermo Vilas, one of the best players in the world through the '70s, won the French and U.S. Opens in 1977. He was also a thoughtful fellow, a serious poet, a very interesting and nice man.

Nonetheless, I remember well a match he played against Borg in the Pepsi Grand Slam Tournament in Florida, where I was doing the television commentary. Someone in the TV booth told me that Vilas had lost to Borg thirty-eight times in a row.

With that information in mind, as the match unfolded, I couldn't believe my eyes. Vilas was playing Borg and staying at the baseline. Nobody could beat Borg by staying at the baseline. True, Vilas had a very strong baseline game, which resembled Borg's in certain ways. He had powerful deep strokes, very heavy topspin. But nobody could beat Borg at his own game as Vilas had demonstrated in the previous thirty-eight times they had met.

"This doesn't make any sense to me," I said.

Somebody in the booth replied, "Well, what should he do?"

"He's got to get into the net," I said. "He's got to change the system in some way."

"Well, Vilas simply doesn't volley that well," the fellow said. "And Borg passes so well."

"Look," I told him. "If you are zero for thirty-eight against Borg, your probability of winning this match is not too great. Especially if you play the same system you used in the previous thirty-eight matches. But what happens if you do go to the net and you begin to guess? You run right. You run left. Now you have changed the game completely, so your chances of winning go up astronomically — maybe 50 percent."

"That may be so," the guy replied, "but Vilas isn't going to do that because it's not his game. He's got to play his game, whatever that is,"

"Well," I said, "I've heard that before and there's a certain amount of truth in it. But if you're zero for thirty-eight and you're going to repeat the game that you played in the previous thirty-eight matches, why don't you just mail in the scores? There's not going to be any change."

By the end of the day, Vilas was 0 for 39.

12. Adapting

I recently broadcast a match between Steffi Graf and Zina Garrison. Zina was up 4–1 in the first set and all of a sudden, on a key point, she looked up and Steffi was at the net volleying away.

After the match, which Steffi won, I interviewed her and she said, "When Zina gets ahead of me, I must come to the net on the right points."

That sounds like a simple enough statement, but Steffi knew that by doing so, she would not only win a point or two, she would also disturb Zina's game plan, attitude, and concentration. And remember, from the baseline, Steffi is enormously powerful. But she knows what's required to win a match. When she's playing at her best, she absorbs data as she plays, then acts upon it. She is a very smart player, which people don't normally give her credit for, and those smarts have enabled her over the years to make adaptations in her game. Her problem at the moment is that she has not been sufficiently adaptive.

That evening of the Graf-Garrison match, I also had an interesting interview with Zina. In the match, she had been up in both sets and she lost them both. Indeed, she has a history of doing that.

So I asked her, "Zina, what do you think happens when you're ahead?"

And she said, in what I think was not only a wonderfully honest but also perceptive analysis of her own game: "The truth is, Vic, I don't have the weapons. I just serve and, you know, my weapon is to get to the net. But if Steffi passes me, well, then I'm dead."

Her analysis could not have been more accurate. She knew that she couldn't stay back and hurt Steffi off the ground. She doesn't have an outstanding forehand or backhand. She knew that she had a game that was good enough to let her beat almost all of the women she plays. It's a game that's good enough to let her get to the finals of Wimbledon, as she did in 1990. But nonetheless, it's a game that is lacking and she knows that if she continues to play only that way, it will take her only so far. It doesn't give her enough room to change and adapt.

I have dreamed of working with Zina for even three days on her ground strokes. She is that close, in my mind, to becoming a hugely successful player.

What's so interesting and exciting to me is that more and more players like Zina are talking in such terms about themselves and their own games. They have better data. They are able to recognize what weapons they have and what they are missing. They also know that if they want to be number one today, they must be good in all departments.

Steffi certainly realizes this. Monica realizes this. Certainly Martina is continually aware of this. You can see it in the ways she has steadily refined and improved her game.

Your own level of play might be somewhat below hers and the others', but the same principles operate.

Honestly analyze your game.

Apply the meaningful data.

CHAPTER 14

Tennis Greats: What They Teach Us

I N T H E PLAY of thirteen of the best tennis players of all time, we can find the key elements of this book. I've selected these players for what they teach us. There may be others that you would put in your own list of all-time greats, but that isn't the exercise here. Rather, I want to discuss the play and attitudes of this selected group in a way that I think will illustrate mental tennis and pull together much of what I've been talking about throughout this book.

Andre Agassi: Mind vs. Talent

To me, Agassi is an extremely interesting and contradictory player.

I first met him in Las Vegas when he was about six years old, and he was already being touted as something of a tennis prodigy. Don Drysdale and I interviewed him for a television show and I put him on my knee and said, "What do you want to be when you grow up?"

And he replied, "Number one."

It's strange, but sometimes with young kids you can tell

that they are going to fulfill their own prophecies. That's how Agassi was. He was born into a tennis family. His father was a tennis pro and his sister later married Pancho Gonzales.

Andre hits a forehand as hard as anybody I've ever seen. It's not that he is blessed with such a powerful, muscular body. He is able to bash the ball as hard as he does because of the way he hits: his stroking patterns are so biomechanically efficient.

In the last few years, he has been doing a lot of well-publicized weight work to build up his body. But that new strength is not what enables him to hit the normal ball even harder. As noted, it will protect his body when he is forced to hit while off-balance, and allow him to hit harder off-balance.

But what gives him his astonishing power is his mechanics. If you watch him hit that forehand, you will see that he coils the length of his body and uncoils it as he spins into the shot, then stops his body at the appropriate point and lets the racket accelerate through the ball. Watch him and you'll see that it's no mystery that he can hit so hard and, in fact, it's a technique that any player can adapt to his own stroke.

His serve is not nearly so bad as many people seem to think. Most people don't know, for example, that in 1988 out of all the players in the world, Andre's percentage for winning second serve points was the highest.

And, after working on the speed of his first serve, Andre was credited in *Tennis Magazine* with hitting the fourth fastest serve in 1991 as measured in fifty IBM/ATP tournaments. Servers in these tournaments were tracked by Information Display Systems and its radar guns and Andre was clocked at 128 mph in Key Biscayne, during the Lipton tournament. He was tied at that speed with Michael Stich of Germany, who with his tremendous serving stunned us all, including the masterful Stefan Edberg in the semifinals of Wimbledon that year, then Boris Becker in the finals. (It was at Wimbledon, incidentally, that the fastest serve of the year was recorded by Marc Rosset of Switzerland at 134 mph, just a blip higher than Andre's.)

Agassi has pretty good court speed but he can learn to volley better. Still, he clearly has real weapons on the court and an extremely powerful game that continues to improve.

Andre's problems, in my opinion, have been largely mental. He appears to be coping with these problems, appears to be maturing, and it is reflected wonderfully in his game and his latest triumphs, most especially, of course, his Wimbledon championship in 1992.

Over the years, he has been wrestling with the demands he places upon himself on the court. He is very tough on himself, and when his game didn't meet his approval, he had a tendency to let it come apart.

We saw this in a number of matches where he got a bad call, or his opponent started to hit harder and better, and before you knew it Andre was walking around punishing himself by playing badly. Right before your eyes, you saw him turn from a dominant player to a struggling one.

I like Agassi personally, and to be honest I cannot say that about all professional tennis players, but I certainly do like him. He is a generous man, a giving kind of person, much of which, obviously, is not public.

In recent years, I think, he has been experiencing a profound mental struggle between his search for personal peace and his public persona, and lately we have been witnessing some resolution of that struggle.

Andre has told me that he is a very religious person. Like Michael Chang, he reads the Bible regularly. He is a believer in God and, quietly and sincerely, he is searching for deeper meaning in his life. I don't know that Barbra Streisand was especially accurate when she called Andre "a Zen master" during the 1992 U.S. Open, but he is a thoughtful searcher and I admire him for that.

At the same time, that side of him has been in direct conflict with his public persona. This is part of his serious inner struggle and his ambivalence. I don't think that Andre has yet completely found himself, as a man or a player. He's just beginning to discover who he is as a player. And as a man, he's growing and maturing, looking.

Still, there seems little question to me that he has resolved a great deal. He shows us on the court a new, impressive level of concentration and genuine toughness. In the finals at Wimbledon, Goran Ivanisevic blasted one ace after another past Andre, precisely the kind of assault before which he used to crumble. No longer. He seemed to transcend it, to retain his own inner-outer focus on his objectives.

After the match, he said he knew that despite the barrage of aces, Ivanisevic was only human. He could not serve an ace on every point, in other words, and he would make mistakes on his ground strokes. He would, like any normal player, give Agassi opportunities to score and those were the qualities he had to keep fixed in his mind and to act upon.

To me, this is all part of Andre's coming to accept himself as a person and a player, rather than a glitzy if extremely lucrative "sideshow."

Working all this out is not easy for anyone, especially if it has to be done in a fairly public way. There, Andre pays the price shared by all hugely successful young pros. If they want to work through meaningful personal matters and problems, they are forced by the nature of their fame to do so in front of everyone, on court and off. They cannot, like average adolescents — and we tend to forget how young some of these players are — work out their evolving personalities in the privacy of more normal worlds and within their families.

Still, out of his maturing process, Andre has become and promises to continue to be an even stronger tennis player. He may or may not change the flashy stuff. I don't know. The outer performance is part of what he and his associates conceive to be his business. It's part of generating attention and media hype that translates into multimillion-dollar product endorsements.

He is still not, then, a person who is at peace with himself. But from my conversations with him, I see a beautiful person within. I like to recall the times when I sat in the stands with him and talked easily about the little things that matter to him. That's very interesting from Andre Agassi. Then I am not hearing the Agassi on the TV commercials who says, "Image is everything." Then what I hear is a young man who thinks a lot about life, about being comfortable with himself and being happy.

He is a tremendous tennis player, who still has vast potential to improve. The improvement is going to finally come, not only from continued work on his strokes — like better volleying and a consistently strong first serve — but when he is able to push further on his inner exploration to a point where he sufficiently understands himself and feels good about who he is and is comfortable with himself.

When that happens, you will see Andre Agassi with a very different mental attitude toward himself, tennis, and all his opponents.

And then he will be an even more difficult player to beat.

Boris Becker: The Importance of Being Selfish

Becker is another player I'm quite fond of and have a great deal of respect for, and not only because of the power of his game and the beauty of his strokes.

Becker was able to transcend a national problem in Germany, and effect an unusual personal, psychological breakthrough. As a teenager, he realized that if he were going to become a world champion, not just a German champion, he was going to have to achieve a level of healthy selfishness. And that he did.

It enabled him to develop his own game, built on his own kind of strokes, not the game that was widely approved and taught at the time by many of the old-line coaches in Germany. When Becker was growing up, Germany had a national system that favored the underspin backhand. It had been taught there for years and in my opinion was one of the reasons there were hardly any Germans in the top world rankings for years. You can't beat world-class players hitting only that essentially defensive stroke.

Becker recognized the limitations of the stroke and the prevalent German system and he and his coach Gunther Bosch created his own, new attacking style, hitting tremendous topspin off both sides.

I give him great credit for that. Not only was he able as a teenager to recognize the limitations in his game, but he was able to develop a new game that violated national dictates.

A teenager, you might say, being the quintessential rebel, would love nothing more than trying to shatter the collective wisdom of the coaching adults of his nation. But Becker's act was hardly one of destructive adolescent trashing. It was a completely positive effort that took vision and strength to accomplish.

In the process, interestingly, he influenced the coaching establishment, enabling a new generation of coaches with new techniques to enter the nation's elaborate teaching system, one reason why Germany is producing so many more world-class contenders today.

Boris's triumph also made things much easier for Steffi Graf. Becker proved that a German could break through. And that was a tremendous lift for her.

Boris also survived the warping public forces that enveloped him when he won Wimbledon as a seventeen-year-old.

First, he became a national hero. When he walked into restaurants in Germany, people stood and applauded. That sudden adulation can dislodge any teenager.

At the same time, he suffered a perverse and punishing media attack. Though he had won Wimbledon and brought international tennis glory to Germany for the first time in decades, when he didn't win every tournament he entered subsequently, and especially when he actually lost at Wimbledon, journalists began writing that he was just a flash in the pan. There was nothing to base that on, as history has demonstrated. But I suppose that the people writing it thought it would sell newspapers and magazines.

Becker was able to rise above all of it. He is a wonderful player, has now won Wimbledon three times, and has been ranked number one in the world, which is not bad for a flash in the pan.

To some degree, his ups and downs are the natural results of the kind of game he plays. He has a style that is tremendously exciting but also dangerous, one that will give him great wins and bad losses. Nevertheless, for all his extremes, he remains a huge threat in every tournament he plays.

Like Agassi, Becker is going through a personal and professional transitional period, improving as a player and maturing as a person. And wrestling with himself.

I don't think we've seen the true Boris yet.

Steffi Graf: Mechanics, Strokes, and Confidence

Steffi is potentially the greatest player in the history of women's tennis. That's my opinion. A lot of people didn't agree with me when I first said it; even more disagree now since Monica Seles has taken the number-one spot away from her.

I think Monica is an absolutely remarkable tennis player, and, as I'll explain later in this chapter, she is transforming the way women play tennis. Yet I still maintain that Steffi has the potential to be the greatest — with one, giant caveat added to this claim: She must be willing and able to make certain specific changes in her game.

But look first at her strengths.

I have never seen a woman who is as strong in her strokes as she is. At times, she can put the ball away from the baseline. That's 78 feet from one end to the other, and in the history of the game there have been only a handful of players who have been able to do that. Frank Kovacs did it on occasion. I've seen Agassi do it. I've seen Becker and Jim Courier do it a few times. Quite recently, I've seen Seles pull it off. But very very few players, men or women, have been able to do that.

To give yourself a sense of just how difficult it is, the next time you're out there playing, try to put the ball away from the baseline yourself. The odds are so heavily against your being able to do it, there aren't any odds. Ken Rosewall couldn't do it. Rod Laver couldn't do it. John Newcombe couldn't do it. Martina Navratilova can't do it. All of them great and powerful hitters. But I have seen Steffi do it repeatedly and she continues to do it.

She also hits an extremely fast serve for a woman or a man. Her service toss and motion aren't the most efficient, but she can still murder the ball.

In 1991, at Wimbledon, she hit a serve 107 mph, the fourth fastest by a woman that year. Bjorn Borg won Wimbledon five times when he was hitting only about 105 mph with his fastest serves.

Until Steffi came along, Martina was the best woman player I had ever seen. Then Steffi appeared, got steadily better, and challenged Martina. Martina met the challenge, improved her own game, played very well. Yet Steffi played even better and began beating her.

During that time, Steffi demonstrated a rare and critical quality, the ability to improve her game, even in the middle of a match.

Now she has to demonstrate that same quality and respond to developments around her, respond flexibly to her competition in a broader way. In order to become number one again, she needs to adjust at least three aspects of her game:

- She has to improve the topspin on her backhand in order to move opponents further out of court, as well as to hit short angled crosscourt passing shots.
- She needs to add a slice to her serve repertoire, so she can keep opponents guessing, and be able to go to the net more often behind her serve.
- She must develop her net game, even if it means missing volleys, to the point where she feels comfortable playing there. Then she will consistently go to the net.

She certainly has the ability to change her style of play. As I said, I have seen her do it with devastating effect in the middle of a match. There she was, banging away from the baseline against Zina Garrison, and all of a sudden she was at the net volleying, at exactly the moment when she needed a point, when she needed to surprise Zina and disrupt her thinking and game plan. She knows how to change the rhythm of a match.

The question, the dilemma I know Steffi is pondering, is whether she can change the style of her play, not just at a given moment in a match, but more completely.

She may not do it. She is, after all, human, and like the rest of us humans, change for Steffi will not be so easy. Further, she might be so extremely comfortable with who she is on the court, with what she is able to do, which after all is a style of play that has served her extremely well, that she may choose, consciously or unconsciously, not to change.

Steffi is still quite young, at present writing only twenty-three years old. Like Becker, she began winning the biggest international tournaments when she was seventeen and eighteen years old. Most people at that age are not overly mature, and that's certainly true of young tennis champions, who lead rather lopsided lives.

To reach that level requires a life in which there is very little else but tennis. They spend all morning, all afternoon, essentially, playing tennis. They don't have much time for an education. Most of the people they associate with are tennis players and coaches and other people who inhabit the tennis world. It is in fact a rather small world. And during the process of growing up in that small world, they are not exposed to much of life that is second nature to other teenagers, which can range from taking care of themselves on streets to understanding why Michelangelo was a great artist. As a result, they are often extremely overdeveloped in their ability to play a sport, but in terms of their broader development, especially their psychological and intellectual development, they are quite underdeveloped.

Not surprisingly, they are extremely underequipped to handle the peculiar stresses of big-time tennis.

Early in Steffi's career, for example, even though she was improving enormously each season, she got no attention. It was all Chris Evert and Martina. Steffi became the third-best player in the world and the media and some tournament officials barely acknowledged her existence.

Quite naturally, that affected her, unquestionably damaged her self-esteem. Even today, she remains resentful of that treatment. It's one of the reasons I think why she is so wary of and sensitive to the media, even walks away from interviewers.

Once in San Diego we had a wonderful session when I began by telling her I didn't want to talk about her strokes because her strokes were already legendary.

"I want to talk about your brain," I said.

She stared at me and laughed. "Nobody's ever asked me anything about my brain before."

In the last couple of years, of course, Steffi has had her

problems, some due to health, some due to a truly distracting media mess her father landed in. For stretches, she has dropped out of the number-one ranking.

Like all great players, she hit a period when the elements of her best game simply did not come together. That happens, just as the best have stretches when they seem invincible.

She tells me that she is now reaching for an all-around game, the game she knows she must possess to regain her crown. She knows that she must improve her volley. While she shows reasonable confidence in her net game against many players, she still seems apprehensive against Monica Seles and Gabriela Sabatini, her two toughest rivals. She is also trying to improve her topspin backhand.

I'm waiting to see if Seles's style will force Steffi to play differently. I do not think Steffi has yet reached the highest level she is capable of reaching. The question of course is whether she will make the changes necessary to reach that level. In my mind, she is still young, still potentially the best player in the history of women's tennis. The very best.

I'm betting that she will make the changes and she will get ever better.

Monica Seles: Where the Amazing Whole Is Greater Than the Parts

Monica Seles plays the game the way no woman has ever played it, and by doing so, she has absolutely changed the game of women's tennis.

I have never seen anyone quite like her. On the backhand side, Jimmy Connors reminds me somewhat of her, the way she can take the ball on the rise, the way she can reduce the time she gives her opponents to react, the way she continually applies pressure. She doesn't allow Steffi or any opponent to get set on their shots.

Martina has likened playing against her and her ferocious strokes to playing against a bazooka. She never allows an opponent to feel comfortable, her concentration, her tenacity, her tempo are so severe. She fights for everything.

Her special brilliance, of which she is aware, lies in that ability to reduce the time opponents have to prepare for their own shots. It enables her to play against people who may have more natural talent than her and to nullify it.

She is also extremely adept at exploiting an opponent's weakness.

Though it is not generally recognized, she does not have a great arsenal of shots, but she moves her feet so well, she compensates greatly. She is able to position herself so that she can hit the ball from the position she wants. If someone hits her a high arching shot, for example, she takes a few quick steps forward so that she can hit it waist-high with a sharp angle.

More than anyone I have ever seen, Monica has forced women pros to reevaluate how they play the game, and they are changing their style of play. She told me recently, "I'm seeing coaches and players improving certain parts of their games specifically to beat me. What I have to do in response is change my own game. I know I must have an all-around game. I must start coming to the net and not give them a chance to manipulate me."

Talking with her, it is clear that she is confronting an inner battle over playing at the net. "I've looked at film of myself as a kid," she told me, "and I had no problem going to the net, and I was good. Now, I am always giving myself excuses not to go."

The battle of course is similar to the one Steffi faces and it involves that difficult matter of change. It is the same challenge Lendl faced at a critical point in his career, when it would have been relatively easy for him to avoid the painful change: he had, after all, been so successful up to that point without any net game. Interestingly, Bjorn Borg was never really forced to deal with it, he was so successful from the baseline. But the game has changed since then and Monica knows that if she stays back, a lot of people will start to beat her.

As I write this, Monica is only nineteen years old, which is to say she has accomplished all she has on the tennis court as a teenager, while off-court she is another example of a young, highly successful woman who is still trying to grow up. She is making mistakes in front of a lot of TV cameras as she does. Her dropping out of Wimbledon in 1991 and the way she handled that are good examples. Yet, we also see change in her, maturity in her. And with it, as with Agassi, we will see an even better tennis player.

Martina Navratilova: Setting Goals

I have tremendous admiration for Martina because she reached the top, dropped back down, applied herself, and became even better.

For a long time, Martina had a bad rap: that she didn't win the big ones. She couldn't seem to win the U.S. Open or a number of other tournaments. Interestingly, this is the same rap her Czech compatriot Lendl got, that they both choked on the big ones.

They both showed their class, however, working passionately at their games until they got to number one. I still use them as models with young players. "Sometimes it might take years to get where you want," I tell them, "but look at these two. Great athletes are willing to do that."

So, for some time she wasn't given full credit for who she was and what she had accomplished. She is a superb athlete and an enormously hardworking woman. I've seen her work out in Aspen, and it's frightening to see the way she pushes herself with weights and other exercises.

She has a fairly complete game, a strong serve, plays

aggressively, comes to the net, but there have been holes in her game. First, there was an underspin backhand. She realized that, and she worked very hard on it. She learned to hit topspin on her backhand, and once she got that stroke, her record improved dramatically.

Martina is absolutely inspiring at setting higher goals for herself. Recently, as I noted, she decided that she had to improve her forehand, to make her game even better. So she worked on it for months and improved it tremendously. "I've been doing nothing but trying to improve that," she told me then.

That is the mark of a very smart tennis player, one who is able to recognize what she has to do, and then applies herself to doing it.

She has strong character. She has had terrible dry spells, going for months and months without reaching the finals of a single major tournament. She has been down and disappointed with herself. Still, at such times, she was strong enough to examine her game and, in a way, step outside herself and objectively look at what was wrong and what she had to do. She changed coaches. She focused on the strokes that had to be improved. She changed her serve.

Once again, I give her enormous credit for a remarkable career. She has won Wimbledon nine times, the U.S. Open four times. And she's still a champion.

I watch some of the women playing today and see how strong and fast they are. Hungry too. And I begin to think, "Wow, any one of these kids can come out and, on a given day, just blow Martina away." But then you get to the semifinals and Martina is there. That happens over and over again.

And life does not get any easier for her. Since she has been at the top as long as she has, everyone guns for her, everyone gears up to play the very best they have ever played when they're up against Martina.

She remains a great champion and a great person.

Chris Evert: Knowing Her Own Game

Early in her career, Chris understood that essential reality I've stressed so in this book — that the ball doesn't care. She was tremendously good at ruling out external stimuli and focusing on the task at hand. She wanted to win. She played every point with the same intensity and concentration. She had great ability as well as enormous tenacity and great patience, which are terribly important for a pro. She was able to stay out there and play. And she could play each point the way it had to be played.

Also, Chris never tried to do more than she was capable of doing. Because of that, many people thought her style of play was boring. But it was extremely intelligent for her. She would not try shots the average player would try, which is to say, silly shots at silly times. Chris never did that and she made very few mistakes. Her father, who was a tennis pro, taught her early, "Let your opponent make the mistakes." And she did just that.

When you watched her you might get the false impression that all she was doing was hitting it back, playing a completely defensive, dull game, indeed a game with the single idea of waiting for her opponent to make mistakes. But, she never got credit for the speed and power she had on the ball. People talk about her as if she were a dinker. But she was a very hard-driving player. More impressively, she hit the ball hard from the baseline, which was her essential game. Players who have played both her and Martina have told me that Chris hit a much harder ball than Martina. Until Steffi Graf came along, she was the hardest-hitting woman in professional tennis.

More than anything, I think of Chris as playing smart tennis. You could beat Chris, but you always had to play well to do so. And that is the mark of a true champion. Can she force her opponents to play their very best in order to beat her? And how often can they play that best? The answer is, seldom. And that is why she won, often.

If there was a flaw in her game, it was, of course, that she never became a volleyer. The truth is that she was a good volleyer, but she never had confidence in herself doing it. I watched her practice from midcourt and play team tennis, and she could hit very crisp volleys. She had good hands. But when she got into singles, apparently she never felt comfortable at the net, so she stuck with her baseline game throughout her career.

I've always said I would give anything to see a match where Chris Evert serves and goes to the net. Or takes service return and goes to the net. I would have killed to see a match like that. And I think she would have been very good playing that kind of style. But obviously she didn't agree.

Chris seemed to keep tennis and life in perspective. Over the years, she grew. And she understood that she had a responsibility to the game of tennis, and especially to young people. She handled herself well on the court.

She is a delightful person, with a very nice sense of humor, not something she demonstrated on the court certainly. But she is great fun to be with and was known to be on the tour.

Unlike some tennis parents you see these days, hers stood for good things. Her mother and father were very supportive. They didn't try to push people around, and that included their daughter. She signed with Wilson sporting goods early in her career and she kept that relationship through her career. Today, according to manufacturers, many pro players have little loyalty to any product. Chris knew what was best for her and she stuck with it. She certainly could have earned more money jumping from one company to another, but she didn't.

She was smart to retire when she did, when she realized that she no longer had the basic qualities she needed to remain on top. She could no longer stay out there with the tenacity of her earlier years, yet her game required tenacity and patience and fortitude. "I don't feel it anymore," she said. And once she knew that, she said, "Okay, I'm going to retire."

Ivan Lendl: Changing with the Data

There was a similarity of sorts between Lendl and Chris Evert. They were both willing to stay out there and do what has to be done in order to win.

I am very fond of Lendl. It always saddened me somewhat that for years he was so unpopular and took such an odd public beating. It seemed that no matter how much he won, he remained unpopular.

He won the U.S. Open, the Australian Open, the French Open, but he couldn't win Wimbledon. So every time he had a press conference, all he got asked about was, "How do you explain that you can't win Wimbledon?"

Clearly, part of Ivan's problem was image. To the average fan, I guess he was not the most exciting player to watch. There was not a great deal of flash about him and/or his game. But I found him tremendously exciting to watch because his execution was perfect. For me, he played a marvelous game.

What I also liked so much about him was that he became number one in the world by sheer determination. He applied himself totally to his profession — playing tennis. He conditioned harder than any other player. He gave up all kinds of pleasures in order to be number one. He suffered the relentless abuse of little people in press conferences. No matter what he did, he couldn't seem to become popular or get crowds on his side. Nonetheless, he persevered and he did indeed become number one in the world.

On his backhand and his forehand, Ivan is as close to a model as anyone can get to the instruction we give at our Tennis College. If you watch him play, you'll see exactly what

I mean. He does not have a big backswing on that forehand. Instead, he loops his racket slightly behind his body and brings it back up toward the ball, a looping motion going from down to up on the ball.

He has worked hard and perfected both those strokes so that they are as strong as those of any player on the tour today. He hits them both with astonishing power and top-spin. Players tell me that they can get blisters from hitting volleys at the net off Lendl's ground strokes. The average player would simply have his racket knocked right out of his hand.

Also, as I said earlier, I give Ivan credit, and many other people have too, for being sufficiently flexible to expand his game. Remember, he reached the top without having any net game at all, without having to hit a lot of volleys. And then he realized that he would not go any further or stay at the top without one. So he began to work on it. It's very difficult to add an entire, major new dimension to your game when you've played as long and as successfully as Lendl had. But he managed to develop a net game and his volleys have gotten strong, firm, and crisp.

I differ with him over his serve. I think he still tosses the ball too high, though that height allows him to put tremendous spin on the ball.

Ivan is extremely intelligent, another quality he's never been given credit for. He has a particular facility for mathematics. I remember one press conference when a number of reporters were saying that Edberg had become the number one player in the world, according to computer rankings. And Lendl told them, "Look, I've got my own computer right here" — pointing to his head — "and this one says he doesn't have the points." And he was right. Edberg did not yet have the points.

I also admire Lendl for the considerable amount of charitable work he has done, quietly. I heard about this from time to time, then we ran a special clinic for wheelchair athletes in Newport Beach, California, and Ivan brought a young crippled child and his mother out from Connecticut so the boy could be part of our clinic. Ivan got no headlines for that because he pointedly asked that he be given no press. And I know of a lot of other charitable work he has done, for which he asked to be kept out of the media.

Jimmy Connors: Every Point the Same

Following Jimmy's life since he was ten years old, I have been intrigued by the way it has been shaped by women. He has spoken of being totally supported by women and for quite a while, he considered his mother his coach.

I remember the first time I ever saw him. It was in Chattanooga, Tennessee. He was just a kid and he was beating another kid in a tournament. It was the other boy's turn to serve, when all of a sudden, out on the court, walked a white-haired, elderly woman with a towel. It was Jimmy's grandmother. She walked over to Jimmy and toweled him off right there on the court in the middle of a game.

His grandmother surely thought she was only doing what a good grandmother should do. But I and the children with me were stunned. The young boy Jimmy was playing didn't know what to say or do. That moment for me seems to illustrate Jimmy and women, all his life.

Interestingly, this same Jimmy was capable of terrible rudeness. He is famous of course for the days when he would give people the finger during a match or grab his crotch, or make other such obscene gestures out on the court.

I get the impression, as he gets older, that he's not so proud of those antics. But he was one of the first players who was allowed to get away with it, to take advantage of the greed that has been built into our professional tennis system.

Rather than throw him off the court for any of his antics, the promoters of tournaments allowed him to do whatever he wanted, because he sold tickets. (They responded in exactly the same manner, of course, to John McEnroe.) In fact, Jimmy used to say: "I give the people what they want," and he was right. To the promoters, that meant the supposed excitement of making obscene gestures in public.

I never bought that. To me, Jimmy sold tickets because of the tennis he played, because of the excitement he created with his racket. To suggest anything else is to trivialize him as a tennis player. After all, when you stop and think about it, is anyone really going to spend good money just to watch a tennis player give an umpire the finger? Why did the crowd go so crazy over Jimmy at the 1991 U.S. Open? He didn't make a single vulgar gesture or statement during the entire tournament, yet the whole place went wild for him. It did, obviously, because of the quality of tennis and the tenacity of spirit he shared with the crowd and the millions who watched on television. It was like a personal gift he offered us all. That is rare, even inspiring. It certainly has nothing to do with the "exciting" behavior of an adolescent.

On the other hand, we can all learn from watching him play. He is a great example of a player who knows that the ball doesn't know or care what the score is. He is famous for playing every point the same way. He knows that you must hit the ball correctly and it doesn't matter what the score is.

To Jimmy's further credit, he was not endowed with a great body for tennis, though he is very fast. He also plays in a way that punishes his feet. His feet roll and take a terrible beating in every match, as do his tennis shoes. My wife, Melody, and I were at the Converse factory one day, and they had a man there who did nothing but work on the 360 pairs of tennis shoes that Jimmy Connors needs every year.

Furthermore, Jimmy does not win anything easily. He works hard. I mentioned earlier in the book how hard he trains when he works out. He goes flat out, a wonderful way to practice.

It's astonishing to me that a person can possess such a bad serve as Jimmy, yet go so far in tennis. As I said earlier, he always disagreed with me about this and reminded me of the number of tournaments he had won.

In the mid-1980s, retained by one of Jimmy's sponsors, Dr. Ariel and I ran a three-dimensional analysis of his serve and his ground strokes. From the perspective of biomechanics, bodily efficiency, physics, and movement, he had the worst serve we ever analyzed of a professional player. The worst.

He also had the best return of serve we ever analyzed.

A lot of players have weak ground strokes, yet they are able to get through some major tournaments by having remarkable serves. Jimmy had no serve of his own, but he was able to take away the weapon of serve-only players because his service returns were so damaging.

I was certainly not alone in my judgment of Jimmy's serve. Countless players told me the same thing. They even joked about it. I remember one top pro joking that the previous night he had suffered his worst nightmare since turning pro. He dreamed that Jimmy Connors aced him.

But these days, you don't hear such jokes. The man who has become the inspirational messiah of middle-aged tennis players has quite appropriately changed his serve. He has lowered his toss, altered some of his mechanics, and now in real life can actually ace an opponent.

I give him enormous credit for that and for sustaining the level of play he has, even at age forty. In my view, if Jimmy had developed a truly strong serve early in his career, he would have won the Grand Slam and compiled one of the most astonishing records in the history of the game.

Bjorn Borg: Smart and Simple

Borg was a marvelous champion and a wonderfully generous man. If anything, he gave too much of himself to the game and to his public.

Borg created an historic breakthrough in tennis for Sweden. He was the first Swede to win on the level he did. And that allowed a whole generation — two generations now — of Swedes to say, "Yes, it's possible for me to be a Swede and to win."

He was extremely generous with himself and his time. Over and over, I saw him trying to eat in a restaurant, people coming up to ask for autographs, and he would always put his food aside and sign. Sometimes I felt sorry for him. I think he never realized that he had a right to say no, that people tended to take advantage of him.

We all know of his remarkable triumphs. No other man in modern times has won five Wimbledon tournaments in a row. Not to mention that he won those tournaments, on grass, while staying on the baseline. That is just an unbelievable feat, a marvelous achievement.

Borg worked hard on his strokes. He really understood how to hit a ball. He stood farther behind the baseline than any other player, but he hit so hard and he hit on such a high parabola with so much topspin that he was extremely difficult to play. He caused the ball to come off the court with so much spin at such a sharp angle and with so much power that opponents had tremendous difficulty getting to the net on him. But even if they got there, his ball was coming back at them so hard and dipping so fast that it was terribly difficult for them to volley against him.

Many players looked as if they were in control against him, but still they missed shots because his return was diving so fast they couldn't hit it back. A lot of players told me that when they volleyed at the net against him, as with Lendl, their rackets rattled in their hands.

There was that great myth about Borg and the way he hit, which I mentioned. People said that he faced the net when he hit the ball, which gave lazy people a terrific excuse for not turning sideways when they hit. But what they seemed to overlook was that, in fact, when Borg hit, he rotated the top of his body tremendously. He rotated his body 110 degrees on his stroke, which meant that he turned his body more on his forehand than other players who turned their whole bodies sideways to the net.

Borg's feet often faced the net, but not the rest of his body. And indeed, that coiling of the top of his body was what gave him such incredible power when he hit his shots.

Borg also had the almost supernatural ability to be late on his backhand side but still hit crosscourt passing shots. It is almost physiologically impossible to do this. A player who is late is essentially bound by his muscle structure to return down the line.

Using high-speed photography on him, I set out to discover how he could do that. What the film showed me was that when he hit his backhand, there was more swelling of the muscle in his left arm than in his right arm. He hit a two-handed backhand, of course. But watching that film I realized that the dominant arm in Borg's backhand was the left one. In other words, it was like a left-handed forehand. I was astonished.

The idea that he was left-handed or that he was hitting a left-handed two-handed shot, or that he might be ambidextrous occurred to me one day in Montreal.

I was up there with Don Drysdale to do a telecast and the day before the match, Borg was working out with a hockey team. He was a good skater and he loved hockey. He was out on the ice exercising and I watched him hitting slapshots. One after another, he hit from the left side. They were good shots too.

And that's when it dawned on me. When you were playing against Borg, you were not playing a right-handed two-handed player. You were playing a right-handed forehand and a left-handed forehand.

Furthermore, when we examined the films closely, we did not find the same swelling of his extensor forearm muscle on his right arm. He was really left-hand dominant on the left side.

Borg had enormous tenacity on the court. He could play forever. Hours and hours and hours. And play each point exactly the way it had to be played, hitting as many balls as had to be hit in order to win. You could beat Borg, but you had to play the very best you ever played to beat him. He was good all the time.

As for strategy, Borg kept the game awfully simple. When asked, he had a standard but accurate response: "Most of the time," he would say, "I hit crosscourt. Every once in a while, down the middle."

In some ways, Borg reminded me of both Ivan Lendl and Chris Evert. He possessed that same kind of wonderful steadiness and solidness, determination, willingness to work, a player who just never quit.

He could adapt his game when necessary. He was number two in the world when he finally realized that he had to strengthen his serve. And he did. He began to throw his ball out more to the right, lowered his toss, and got a lot more power behind it. It became a much greater weapon for him.

It saddens me somewhat that Borg has had a rather difficult time with his life since leaving tennis. He is such a quality man I'm sorry that his various business ventures didn't seem to work out, his marriage and relationships with women were so stormy. And his attempts to play pro tennis again have not yielded much.

Yet, he remains such a class man and was such a wonderful champ that anybody connected with tennis as I am must be forever indebted to him.

John McEnroe: Genius and the Effects of Anger

As a tennis player, McEnroe has done about as much as anybody I've ever seen. He has the best hands of any player I've ever seen. And he's astonishingly creative. When he was playing well, he was just unbelievable. He could take a half volley at his feet and put it away.

He was an absolute genius at knowing where the racket head had to be and capable of taking the toughest shot and making it good. Further, he was remarkable at knowing what shot to hit at just the right time and being able to hit it.

I remember in 1981, before his greatest match at Wimbledon, which was against Borg, I said that if they got into a tiebreaker, McEnroe would win it. Some writers took exception to that. But sure enough, McEnroe did win one of Wimbledon's greatest battles in the fifth set, in a tiebreaker.

Of course, when you make a prediction like that, some of it is just guessing. But on the other hand, in crucial points on grass, the player in control of the net has a greater chance of winning in my view.

Furthermore, I knew McEnroe had all the shots, and was never afraid to hit the shot that had to be hit. An awful lot of players, even at the highest pro levels, don't have the confidence and the guts to do that. Under stress, they regress to conservative playing. But McEnroe never did. He was absolutely brilliant at delivering that big shot under tremendous stress.

I suppose that because he had such phenomenal ability I expected that much more of him as a man and as a human being.

First of all, as wonderful as he has been for tennis, in the pure sense of playing it, he has also been a terrible role model.

When I'm out working with children, I tell them that "Great champions are ones who can keep their cool, like Bjorn Borg. They don't crack, give in to the pressures of the moment." And an eleven-year-old kid says, "Excuse me, McEnroe is my hero and he's swearing at everyone on the court!" And soon you see the kid swearing and throwing his racket.

Now, obviously, each child and his family ultimately bear responsibility for the child's behavior. But McEnroe gave credibility to the idea that a champion can be rude and crude, and still win. That if you are a champion, and you're good enough, you can act with impunity, no matter what you do.

It isn't a matter of simple anger. Everyone has a right to angry feelings. When it comes to tennis, we all have matches where we feel an umpire is robbing us and we get angry. The problem for adults, at least, in tennis and in society at large, is how we deal with these emotions.

McEnroe never felt he had to restrain his feelings or curb them in deference to anyone. And, indeed, there are those who argue that this explosive side of his personality helped him play better, helped him cope with the exceptional pressures on a top player — a combative media, a fickle crowd, manipulative tournament officials, as well, of course, as the pressure of playing for huge stakes.

And, he was allowed to indulge those attitudes, not only get away with outrageous personal behavior, but do so to his own advantage. Such behavior, of course, disturbs the concentration and play of any opponent. And it upsets and intimidates linespeople or umpires who are involved in the match.

Such behavior also, unfortunately, gave McEnroe a great sense of control. When he started throwing his tantrums and no one stopped him, he knew then he controlled the match.

He also knew that professional tennis had a great deal of hypocrisy about it. There were plenty of rules, but if you sold enough tickets, you could do anything. Nobody was going to throw you out of a match, certainly, just because you started screaming obscenities at an umpire or fans, or breaking your racket or anything like that. Certainly not if you were John McEnroe and people paid good money to see you play.

To the contrary, in a piece of sad irony, when McEnroe

was finally thrown out of his first major tournament, the Australian Open in 1990, all it really meant for him was that he could probably get another $10,000 on top of the $50,000 to $75,000 that he usually gets for any exhibition match.

It did have some effect, if not on him personally. But he knew that under the new pro rules he had to watch his step or he could collect additional penalty points and be prohibited from playing in further big tournaments during the year. But it never affected his personality or his attitude.

In his own defense, McEnroe has said that people are simply envious of him. And to a certain degree, that's true and that's why they attack him. Many people would like to have what he has. He can go anywhere, do anything, buy any house. He can get $50,000 or more for an exhibition match that is merely a pleasant workout for him. So a lot of people are envious. But it seems obvious to me that there is much much more to McEnroe and the criticism that he has received over the years.

McEnroe is the E.T. of tennis. In a sad way, he comes from another planet and has talents and abilities that transcend all but a few earth-dwellers, and indeed he has been treated as if he were from another planet.

In some ways I thought he was like a child, our child, the most gifted kid in our family. And maybe because he was so gifted, we never placed any limits on him, we never set any boundaries on his behavior. Instead, we encouraged his tantrums, his disobedience. And, alas, we got what any child psychiatrist might have predicted.

In the end, I guess, it's that that has been most destructive for McEnroe and for tennis. I think we have to ask the question, "Why should McEnroe not have behaved the way he has?" For acting as he did, he has not suffered anything. He has only made more money. Official tennis and the rest of us have done everything that we could to reward him for his behavior. And McEnroe learned very early on that money talks. He learned that he was more powerful than the rules. And that's all quite sad. Ironically, perhaps, we owe him an apology for letting him get away with what he has, because a man's character is much more important than any tennis match.

Tennis today still needs his genius.

Rod Laver: Hitting What Had to be Hit

Rod was the only player in the history of tennis to win all four Grand Slam tournaments — the U.S. Open, the Australian Open, the French Open, and Wimbledon — in one year and to accomplish that sweep twice, in 1962 and 1969.

Of all his outstanding qualities, the one that rises above the others was his great ability like McEnroe's to know exactly what shot the moment required and to hit it. Once again, it was a question for Rod of always playing the ball. No matter how far ahead he was in any match or how far down he was, he always focused on the necessary shot.

Rocket, as he was called, was able to keep his game at the highest level throughout his career. A reputation for a kind of invincibility evolved about him and he became aware of it. He knew the self-doubt that this reputation placed in the minds of most of his opponents. And he also knew that its greatest impact would occur in long matches and tiebreakers. That is why he loved a match when it got close and why he won so many long matches and tiebreakers.

Rocket would seize the moment, always playing to win. The best athletes in all sports share those qualities. The greater the pressure, the more they respond to it. In basketball, we see superstars like Michael Jordan who love to get the ball with only seconds remaining on the clock, the whole game riding on their one last shot. Players who aren't quite so good end up setting picks for the Michael Jordans. Rod Laver was a player who relished those moments.

Rod sustained a nice perspective on life and possessed a fairly even disposition on the court and off. That helped him play well under pressure. While he certainly wanted to win, he knew that life and death did not hang in the balance. For many players, there is no life if they cannot win.

His perspective and equilibrium allowed him to be somewhat disengaged during a match, the same quality that enabled him to concentrate so totally on the ball and on the shot he had to hit. He was not distracted by psychological problems involving his opponent, or the pressure of the moment. He eliminated all of that. He was a splendid example of what can happen if you shed psychological baggage when you play.

Ken Rosewall: Smart and Beautiful

Rosewall was living proof that you don't have to be a powerful linebacker to be a great tennis player. He was slight, only about 5'7". Naturally, he was nicknamed "Muscles." He did, however, have very strong arms and legs and kept his weight constant, as he has all through his life. At the age of fifty-four, he was only one pound heavier than he was as a senior in high school.

Rosewall developed extremely beautiful strokes. I remember before tournaments, players who were warming up stopped when Rosewall came out to hit. He was such a graceful player, they wanted to watch him.

Michael Davis, who played in the Davis Cup for Great Britain and is now an executive officer of the International Tennis Association, told me that he hated to play Rosewall, but he loved watching him. Too much. It was extraordinary, he said, in matches against him, he caught himself at times not playing but becoming a spectator. And actually found himself saying, softly, out loud, right in the middle of a match, things like, "God, look at him stay over the ball. . . . Look how perfect he is on each stroke."

One of the important keys to Rosewall's game was a fact few were aware of: Rosewall, who hit all of his lovely strokes right-handed, was a natural left-handed player. Even today, he plays golf left-handed.

When he was young, his father switched him to right-handed because he thought that Ken would be a better tennis player that way. Being a natural left-handed player, he had, like Borg, the strengths of an ambidextrous player.

He told me that if he had to do it over again, he would serve left-handed and play ground strokes right-handed. That might have made him the greatest player in the history of the game. He would have been even tougher to beat than he was, and as it was, he was pretty close to unbeatable for a number of years.

Jack Kramer talking about him made the point that in tennis, the higher your competition, the more important speed and anticipation become, and Rosewall was wonderfully fast and showed a splendid sense of anticipation.

His forehand was weaker than his backhand. Gonzales always said, however, that he had to be careful because while he would normally start out playing to Muscles's forehand, that forehand got better and better as the match progressed. Gonzales became quite good at picking up when Rosewall was becoming grooved on his forehand.

He had a very good volley and an unbelievable backhand volley. It was actually better than the forehand volley of most pros. Not surprisingly, he was a strong doubles player with good approach shots, a good net game, and of course solid ground strokes.

Unquestionably, he had one of the best backhands in the history of tennis. It was almost flat and it was very precise. As Mike Davis observed at his peril, Ken stayed over the ball, perfectly. And if you served to his backhand, amazingly he could take it crosscourt or go down the line, whatever he wanted.

He was an absolutely brilliant analyst of the game, though he didn't talk a lot about his own game or strategies.

I remember once, though, talking to him about Nastase, who always looked so fast to everybody. I was recalling one particular match and how it seemed remarkable that Nastase could get to some of those balls. Ken assured me that Nasty made it look better than it really was.

What I hadn't picked up but Rosewall had was that Nastase had a trick of overplaying on one side. He would leave the other side open, knowing that his opponent was going to go for it. Then he would steal a head start. He always brought the crowd to its feet because no one thought he had any chance to reach the ball. Well, Rosewall was not fooled. Whenever he played Nastase, he would return the ball to the point where Nastase had been when he made his initial hit.

He was smart in other ways, as well. I mentioned his serving exercise, his way of loosening his muscles in preparation for a match. He would always come out swinging his racket in a slow overhead motion. Before he ever got on the court, he had taken a hundred or so service motion swings. Ken never had any shoulder problems.

Like his friend Rod Laver, he was even-tempered when he played, not an up-and-down emotional player. And he was masterful at ruling out the past and focusing on the present. Once again, he took each ball hit by hit and did exactly what he felt was needed to that ball.

Ken was very very careful with his money, but he was personally very generous with himself when it came to tennis and especially in supporting professional tennis.

I don't think many people realize how indebted the game is to Ken Rosewall. Time after time, when Jack Kramer was running the tour, he had to turn to Ken and ask him to fly back from Australia to fill in for yet another player who bowed out of yet another event. This was after Ken had already traveled on the tour for maybe forty weeks out of fifty-two.

Pro tennis was on the ropes at that time. Rosewall always responded, sacrificing a great deal of his own time and family life to help us out. If it hadn't been for him, I think it's safe to say that pro tennis might well have died. That kind of commitment to tennis and helping people out is something that is so rare today.

Jack Kramer: The Complete Game

Jack was the best player I've ever seen.

Don Budge, who Kramer called the greatest player in the history of the game, was indeed a superb player. But Jake had the best all-around game. He could hit the ball deep. And he had the best approach shot I've ever seen. Remember, after serve and service return, the approach shot is the third biggest shot in the game. On his approach shot, Jake would lay the ball way back into the corner and it faded, especially on the forehand side. That meant his opponent was hitting a lot from inside the alley.

Jake was lethal when he got close to the net. He was rangy, had nice movement and great anticipation. It was almost impossible to pass him. And he didn't make many mistakes.

People always talked about him winning off of his big serve, as if all he had was a big serve and a volley. Understandable, since in a way, he brought that game to the world. But in fact, he was also remarkable from the baseline. He told me that he could not remember ever losing on clay to Pancho Gonzales. Think about that.

On their famous head-to-head tour he beat Gonzales 96–27. If you beat somebody as good as Gonzales ninety-six times, you have to be an extraordinary player.

He was good from back, good from up front, he had a big serve and a good approach shot. When you've got all that, it means you're a winner.

Jake also had the ability that all great champions share — to concentrate totally on the match at hand. He could be playing in the fifth set, 4–4, with his opponent serving well. And then finally the guy throws in a soft second serve. Jake has pounced on it almost before it has hit the ground, followed it up to the net, and put it away. He had been waiting for his opponent to hit a soft second serve for two hours. He hardly ever let an opportunity go by.

As an analyst, he was unparalleled. He could watch a player once and tell you exactly how to beat him. I talked to countless players who told me that Jack had zeroed in on exactly the flaws that guaranteed he would beat them.

He was tough. Gonzales could intimidate most of his opponents, but that stuff never touched Jake. I recall once when another pro, not nearly so good as Gonzales, tried to psych Jake in the locker room before their match. The guy kind of snuck up on Jake and started to tell him why Kramer was going to lose tonight. He was quite forceful about it, too.

Jake heard him out, never taking his eyes from the guy's face. "Okay," he said, "now let me give you a few good reasons why you're going to take gas. First, you've got no serve, a lousy forehand, a lousy backhand, and a terrible net game. And, second, whenever people are nervous before playing me, they always talk a lot."

Kramer practiced somewhat the way Connors did, hard under assumed game conditions. And when he started to lose his concentration, he would stop. He never did anything in a haphazard way.

For all his analytic brilliance, he was never intellectual about tennis. He could break down a game and point out a player's weaknesses, but over and over I had exchanges with him regarding studies we had done at the tennis college, and our discussions always turned out the same.

I recall one such typical exchange when I said, "Jake, you know I did a study on the trouble players have using a backhand grip on service return, and changing from backhand to forehand. It's fascinating what we found out."

"I don't know anything about science, kid," he said, "but if I'd see guys playing with their backhand grip, I always served right into their body. And I always nailed them. Why? Because for most people it takes longer to go from a backhand to a forehand grip."

He knew it. He didn't have any interest in research, but he knew it. He often said to me, "You think about it, kid, and I'll go out there and play it."

He was brilliant on the court and very smart off the court. He could even add three columns simultaneously in his head.

He was a very decent man who was loyal to people and always helped people who needed it. But when he got on the court, he could divorce himself from such nice qualities and focus totally on what needed to be done.

I found Jake extraordinary as a man and as a human being. I worked closely with him for fifteen years and our friendship has lasted for nearly forty years. He had a set of principles and he stuck with them, some of which got him into trouble.

He was the first player to stand up and say, "I've been taking money under the table and it's not right." That was back in the days when amateurs or so-called amateurs were being paid under the table to play in tournaments. Everybody knew it. Nobody said anything about it. The people running amateur tennis at the time were hypocrites. And Jake finally decided that it simply wasn't right. He was in favor of open tennis and was willing to stand up and say so.

A lot of important people got mad at him for saying what he did and doing what he did, and they tried to ruin his career by keeping him out of tournaments. He knew the risks involved in what he was doing, but he felt it was the only correct thing to do.

He also believed as I do that tennis champions have a responsibility to be good role models. Connors and McEnroe used to say, "Just judge me for my tennis." But, life is more complicated than that. Children look up to them, so Jack felt strongly that it was not enough for them or any tennis champions simply to hit a big serve and have a strong net game.

Sure, he said, you can look at them for their tennis, but that doesn't mean we can be blind to their behavior. And he was quite vocal about it. He said to me once, "Look, what McEnroe is doing is wrong. What Jimmy Connors is doing is wrong. People should be able to win for their tennis ability, not for manipulating emotional levels of other players. They should be good models." And he was right.

He was a wonderful model himself, always courteous. He grew up in a very modest family. His father, who worked on the railroad for Union Pacific, and his mother were great influences on him.

Jake told a story about himself and his father and I think it tells us a lot about Jake and his personality as contrasted with some of the behavior we have seen in recent years.

When he was young, just starting to play, he was in a tournament at the Los Angeles Tennis Club. His father was watching the match from outside the fence. The umpire began to call a lot of foot faults that Jake thought were wrong. He got angry, started to yell, and threw his racket over the fence.

His father picked up the racket, walked on to the court, and talked to the umpire.

Jake went back to the fence and just waited and thought, "That's my dad. He's gonna give this guy what he deserves."

His father finished talking to the umpire, and the umpire stood up and said, "Game, set, and match to Smith!"

His father had just defaulted Jake. His father had told the umpire that no child should be allowed to behave that way on a tennis court during a match, and anyone behaving that way should be defaulted. "Don't ever embarrass yourself," his father said to him afterward, "or your father."

Jake was extremely generous with himself, giving advice and strategy freely to players. I remember once he came out of semiretirement and even suffering from terrible arthritis, he beat Ken Rosewall. Then after the match, he took Ken aside and analyzed the whole match for him.

The arthritis, which started to affect him even in his twenties and became progressively worse, never kept him from charity matches. After one of those, I was talking with him while he was toweling off, and his doctor came in to give him a shot to help cut down the pain. I knew he had arthritis, but I had no idea it was that bad.

"Kid, if you put a thousand-dollar bill on my knee right now," he said to me, "I could not bend down to get it."

Yet he was out there playing.

It was for a good cause and it was for tennis.